Seven Days
in
Sydney

Manly hydrofoil on Sydney Harbour.

David Messent

Published by
DAVID MESSENT PHOTOGRAPHY
Telephone Sydney 971 5970
First Edition Published 1988
Revised and updated 1989

Copyright
National Library of Australia
ISBN No. 07316 1782 7

Text   : David Messent & Graham White
Design   : Ian Richards
Photography : David Messent
Helicopters : Heli-Aust
Maps   : Premier Maps Sydney
Typesetting : Deblaere Typesetting Pty Ltd
Assembly   : Max Peatman

Colour Separations: Sinnott Bros. Sydney.
Printed by Singapore National Printers

Following page: Moonrise over the Opera House.

Seven Days

Contents

Introduction

Sydney has recently turned 200 years old. Just a baby compared with Rome, Athens, Tokyo, Moscow or any other major city you care to mention. Yet what our city has to offer eclipses any other traditional tourist destination in the world. True, we may not have a Colisseum or a Parthenon, but we do have a fascinating colonial history. This history is not bound up in mystery and legend, but is right there to be examined for the asking; the journals of First Fleet sailors and the despatches of the first Governors can be viewed on micro-film at the Mitchell Library and the State Archives, while houses, stores, churches and public buildings dating from the first decades of the colony still exist in Sydney.

Anyway, who needs a Parthenon when we've got the Opera House. Surrounded on three sides by sparkling blue water, its white sails glistening in the sunshine, the Opera House stands on its own as an example of modern architecture. Try to think of another modern building to compare it with and you'll see what I mean. Then there's the Harbour Bridge; still the widest steel arch bridge in the world; it identifies Sydney as surely as the name on an atlas. But the bridge and Opera House would be nothing without Sydney Harbour, Sydney's raison d'être. 'To see Sydney Harbour' is the reason most tourists give for visiting Sydney.

Forget muggings in New York and civil strife elsewhere, Sydney is a safe place to visit. Forget snow in Montreal and drizzle in London, Sydney's climate is pleasant throughout the year. Summers are warm to hot, winters are mild, spring and autumn are perfect, while rainfall comes in short sharp bursts so most days are sunny. Forget Cannes, Malibu, Rio and Waikiki, Sydney's beaches, in particular the 13 beaches on the Pacific Ocean between Manly and Palm Beach, are the best in the world. And forget Paris cuisine. Sydney's restaurants are excellent and cater for every conceivable taste at locations from Rasputin's Russian Restaurant to the Woolloomooloo Woolshed.

When it comes down to it you don't go to see a city to lie on the beach or sit in a restaurant, but to see the sights, which I hope this book will help you to do. Most tourists visit Sydney for a week or less, so I've covered the most interesting places to visit if you only have seven days to spare. All the tours start and finish at Circular Quay, which is served well by ferries, trains, buses and taxis and is within walking distance of most of Sydney's major hotels. The tours for Tuesday and Thursday are easier if you have a car, but they can be done on public transport. Bus and train maps of Sydney are available at most newsagents. So start each day on Map 5 at Circular Quay, refer to the grid on maps 1 and 2 for adjoining maps, and enjoy your stay in Sydney!

David Messent

1

MONDAY

Harbour scenery and Australian wildlife

Walk through The Rocks and up Bridge Stairs to the Harbour Bridge, then climb to the top of the Pylon Lookout for a magnificent view of Sydney Harbour. After crossing the bridge, a cab ride takes you via North Sydney to an old gun battery at Bradley's Head. Following a short harbourside walk and a visit to the zoo, return to Circular Quay by ferry.

Sydney Harbour Bridge

I guess there couldn't be a more logical point to start a tour of Sydney than with the *Harbour Bridge*. Dominating Sydney's skyline since it was completed in 1932, the Bridge has become an unofficial symbol of Sydney to people all around the world, while its pedestrian footpath and south-east pylon provide a vantage point for spectacular views of the city, Opera House and harbour.

Follow the pavement on the west side of Circular Quay past the brown sandstone building which previously belonged to the Maritime Services Board. This is the Museum of Contemporary Art – one of Australia's major collections of modern art, representing the work of over 500 artists from around the world including Henry Moore and Picasso. Turn left up Argyle Street. Stay on the north pavement of Argyle Street for 200 metres, and ascend Argyle Steps to your right near a concrete Bridge over the road. At the top of the steps turn left on the path into Cumberland Street and cross over to *Bridge Stairs* that lead up to the pedestrian footway of the Harbour Bridge.

For many years the Harbour Bridge was only floodlit on the eastern side, but the people in the west of Sydney complained, "Why don't we get to see the bridge under floodlights," so in 1985 the Department of Main Roads attached floodlights to the west side of the bridge also. Here's the west side (below) floodlit in all its glory shortly after the job was completed.

8

It was due to be an historic occasion. The Cunard Liners Queen Elizabeth II and Saga Fiord were arriving off Sydney Heads at the same time and were going to steam together two abreast through the Harbour. However, because of strong winds, for safety reasons it was decided the ships should navigate the Harbour one at a time. Here's the Saga Fiord passing beneath the Harbour Bridge. (above left)

A bird's eye view of Sydney Harbour Bridge. (below left)

The top of the arch of the Harbour Bridge (left) is 134 metres (440 feet) above the water. It was the tallest construction in Sydney from 1932 until 1967 when the Australia Square Tower was completed. On hot days the top of the arch rises an extra 18 centimetres as the bridge heats up and expands.

Part of the lattice (above) of 52,000 tons of steel contained in the arch. When the bridge was opened the toll was 6d per passenger in a car, 3d for motorcycles or for a horse and rider, 2d per head of cattle and 1d per head of sheep or pigs. The Harbour Bridge is not the longest steel arch bridge in the world, but it is listed in the Guinness Book of Records as the widest, with a deck 49 metres wide.

The Rocks area of Sydney (previous pages), is sandwiched between the south approach to the Harbour Bridge and the liner Canberra, berthed at the Overseas Passenger Terminal at Circular Quay. The Canberra is just too high to fit beneath the Harbour Bridge. Once when the ship was backing out of Circular Quay, its mast snagged on the deck of the bridge.

The colonial style North Sydney Post Office and Courthouse (right) was once the tallest building in North Sydney, and could be seen for miles in all directions. Now it's hemmed in by skyscrapers.

The quaint St Peter's Church and Vicarage (below) at North Sydney.

Sydney from Lavendar Street, North Sydney (above right). The picture was taken during the Bicentennial Naval Review, when civilian aircraft took part in a low level fly past over the city.

Sydney from North Sydney at dusk. (below right)

Previous pages. The Opera House, with the Manly Ferry 'Freshwater' passing by, taken from the Harbour Bridge.

13

On the roadway at the top of the steps, the opening ceremony for the Bridge was turned into a fiasco on March 19, 1932, when *Francis de Groot,* an Irish member of the New Guard, slashed through the opening ribbon with his sword before the Premier of New South Wales could cut it with his scissors. The New Guard was a private anti-communist organisation, which didn't like the idea of the Labor Premier of New South Wales Jack Lang, opening the Harbour Bridge. One of the members of the New Guard, Captain Francis de Groot, donned his old Hussar regiment uniform and followed the Governor's escort on horseback onto the Bridge. Nobody took any notice of de Groot on the Bridge and he waited patiently through the opening speeches for his cue, when he spurred his horse forward and cut through the ribbon, when it was stretched across the road, with his sword.

De Groot was bundled off his horse, arrested and charged, and at his trial found guilty of offensive behaviour in a public place and of injuring government property ... 'to wit one ribbon', and fined five pounds with four pounds costs. In his last known statement about the affair before he died in 1969 in a Dublin nursing home, de Groot said, 'I had opened the Harbour Bridge and that was all that mattered.'.

From the walkway you can look down on *The Rocks* area of Sydney, the first part of Australia settled by Europeans when the first fleet arrived in 1788; or at least what is left of it; 300 buildings were demolished in The Rocks when the Harbour Bridge and approaches were built. On the Bridge itself a constant stream of traffic passes by. During the rush hour 15,000 vehicles sometimes cross the Bridge every hour, over double the estimated maximum capacity of 6,000 an hour calculated when the Bridge was designed. The two traffic lanes next to the walkway carried trams until 1958, when the lines were pulled up and the new road lanes opened in July 1959.

The Pylon Lookout

The walkway soon leads you to the south-east example of one of the 'Pillars of Hercules bestriding the tide', as The Sydney Morning Herald in 1932, dubbed the pairs of pylons gracing both ends of the Bridge. The hollow 89 metre high pylons, constructed from 18,000 cubic metres of granite quarried at Moruya on the south coast of New South Wales, are aesthetic and serve no particular structural purpose. A steel staircase through the inside of the pylon leads up to a display area with photos of the construction of the Bridge and examples of the rivets and steel used in fabrication. An open air observation lookout is right at the top. The pylon is open every-day from 9.00 am to 5.00 pm and entry is free.

Walk across the Harbour Bridge, through the north west pylon and down the steps near Milsons Point railway station to Broughton Street. If you're feeling hungry after the climb over the Bridge, walk to Kirribilli Seafoods near the corner of Fitzroy Street. In a section on 'The Best in Australia' in the Sydney Morning Herald's Good Weekend Magazine in 1986, Kirribilli Seafoods was included as the best fish and chips shop and with prices starting at $2.60 it is great value.

Aerial view of the city (above left) with North Sydney in the foreground.

The Lower North Shore suburbs (above) with Manly and North Head in the distance.

Neat stone trenches (right) connect the gun emplacements.

'Victoria Regina' 1871 (above), neatly inscribed in the stonework.

When the gun batteries at Bradleys Head (top) were completed in 1871, they had a clear line of fire to the Harbour. Now the view is obscured by trees. The Russian Pacific Fleet was considered the biggest threat at the time.

The main entrance to Taronga Zoo. (top)

The harbourside track at Bradleys Head (left).

The cuddly koala (above). This one is at the Koala Park at West Pennant Hills in Sydney, where you can get closer to the animals than at the Zoo.

The Giraffe Enclosure at Taronga Zoo.

Harbour Views

Turn left out of the fish and chip shop, stroll up Fitzroy Street and right into Jeffrey Street. Walk down to the water's edge to Cope's Lookout and Jeffrey Street Wharf which was opened by the Honourable John L. Waddy, Member for Kirribilli, on 24 September 1969. Sit down on one of the benches facing the water, and while you're enjoying the best fish and chips in Australia, feast your eyes on Australia's best view; the panorama of the Opera House, city, Sydney Harbour and the Harbour Bridge.

If you are feeling a little more energetic, walk up Kirribilli Road, turn right into Waruda Avenue, then right again into Waruda Street where you will find Mary Booth Reserve. The reserve was named after Dr Mary Booth, a militant feminist, born in 1868, who believed that "good wives make good husbands"!

Go back the way you have come continuing down Kirribilli Road.

Just past Jeffrey Street Wharf you will see on your left the construction works for Sydney's Harbour Tunnel. When completed in August 1992, it is expected the Tunnel will increase the Harbour's crossing capacity by 50 per cent and save 10 minutes travelling time per crossing. Being built by a joint venture, incorporating the Australian company Transfield and the Japanese company Kumagai-Gumi, the Tunnel will operate privately until 2022 when it will be handed over to Government authorities.

On your right is Bradfield Park, named after Dr John Job Crew Bradfield, who was appointed in 1912 to oversee construction of a harbour crossing. Walk along Olympic Drive beneath the Harbour Bridge and turn right into Alfred Street.

North Sydney

Hail a cab on Alfred Street, turn left along Lavender Street, right into Blues Point Road and Miller Street, then sharp right down the Pacific Highway. At the top of Blues Point

Road there is a neat little sandstone church and vicarage, *St. Peters.* On the corner of the Pacific Highway and Miller Street stands the white Victorian colonial style *North Sydney Post Office,* while on the opposite corner occupying an old bank building, reposes the 9,000th McDonalds restaurant in the world, opened in February 1986.

Cross the overpass at the end of the Pacific Highway over the Bradfield Highway, turn left at the traffic lights at Clark Road and follow the road around *Anderson Park* into Kurraba Road. The pioneer aviator *Kingsford Smith* once landed his bi-plane and took off again from Anderson Park during a flight across Australia.

Neutral Bay at the end of the park received its name in 1789, when Governor Phillip ordered that all foreign ships stopping in Sydney must anchor in 'Neutral Bay'. On the southern side of the bay, two or three Oberon Class submarines can usually be seen moored at HMAS *Platypus,* a submarine base commissioned in 1967 at the Australian Navy's torpedo repair and maintenance depot.

Bradley's Head

Follow the map through the back streets of Sydney's Lower North Shore suburbs, pass the Zoo into the virgin bushland of *Ashton Park,* then pay off the cab driver when the road reaches the old fortifications at *Bradley's Head.* Entry to the park is free during the week, but there is a small fee per car at weekends.

Three cannons mounted on carriages in gunpits at Bradley's Head are the best preserved example of a series of fortifications that were built on Sydney Harbour headlands during the 1870s.

Bradley's Head, named after Lieutenant William Bradley, a cartographer with the First Fleet who went on to become a Rear Admiral, was the first of Sydney's harbourside military reserves to be handed over for public recreation in 1908.

Descend the steps on the other side of the road from the cannons, which take you down to the harbour foreshore, where a ship's mast stands above the remains of some more old gunpits. The mast, from the cruiser HMAS *Sydney,* is a memorial to four men killed in action in the battle of the Cocos Islands on September 9, 1914. During the battle, the first in which a ship of the Royal Australian Navy took part, the Sydney sank the German raider 'Emden' and captured her crew. A stone pillar on the rocks just in front of the mast is one of the columns from the facade of the old Sydney G.P.O. building demolished in 1875. Between 1875 and 1912 ships ran speed trials between *Fort Denison,* a small fort that can be seen on an island in the direction of the Opera House and the pillar on Bradley's Head, which is exactly one nautical mile, until it was decided the practice posed a danger to other shipping.

Bush Walks

At the end of the carpark on Bradley's Head, follow the path past the galvanised steel fence. Continue on the path for about a kilometre, through unspoilt bushland with views on the left across the harbour to the city and several decommissioned navy ships tied up at a jetty close by. When the path reaches the road, follow the road downhill for about 200 metres to the *cable car,* which takes you on a two-and-a-half minute ride over the hippos and alligators to the top entrance to *Taronga Zoo.*

Taronga Zoo

Taronga is aboriginal for 'beautiful view', and I think that, without question, everyone would agree Taronga Zoo on its location overlooking Sydney Harbour, is the most beautiful Zoo site in the world. Buy a copy of the Taronga Zoo guide and map at the shop near the entrance and search out some of Australia's unique wildlife. Koalas, Kangaroos, Emus, Wombats, the Duck-billed Platypus and many examples of antipodean birds, reptiles and sea creatures, can all be found. There are also the every day rhinos, big cats, apes and bears that help make up Taronga Zoo's total collection of 4,000 mammals, birds, reptiles and fish.

The Zoo is open from 9.00am to 5.00pm, although visitors can stay until sunset. As far as it can, the Zoo tries to be self-supporting, and you will notice the names of companies and individuals on many of the cages who sponsor the animals.

Exit by the lower entrance to the Zoo and walk down the hill to the wharf at the bottom of the road, from here a regular ferry service runs to Circular Quay. When Taronga Zoo opened in 1916, the animals including Jessie the elephant, were shipped across the harbour from the old Moore Park Zoo by vehicular ferry and offloaded at the wharf.

Tonight, wander to The Rocks to enjoy a drink in one of the old pubs. If you are eating out, the Waterfront Restaurant or the Imperial Peking Harbourside, in Campbell's Storehouse, with a view across Circular Quay to the Opera House, would be hard to beat for atmosphere and a first class meal. Bookings for the Waterfront Restaurant are on 27 3666, bookings for the Imperial Peking Harbourside are on 27 6100.

TUESDAY

Stately buildings and famous Bondi Beach

Journeying by car to the University, then Victoria Barracks, we go through the terraced houses of Paddington, and onto Bondi Beach, before visiting The Gap, Watson's Bay, Vaucluse House and returning to Sydney.

At the east end of Circular Quay, turn up Phillip Street, cross Chifley Square into Elizabeth Street and follow it down to the south end of Hyde Park, where, if you've made an early start, you should be able to find a parking spot at one of the parking meters. Make sure that you leave your hotel with a pocketful of $1 coins, Sydney's parking meters have a voracious appetite.

Hyde Park

In the centre of Hyde Park stands the *Sydney War Memorial* and Pool of Remembrance. The building of the Memorial was financed by 60,000 pounds collected from a fund opened on April 25, 1916, the first anniversary of the landing of Australian and New Zealand troops at Gallipoli. Following a design competition the memorial was planned and constructed by Sydney architect Bruce Dellitt, with the sculptures the work of Raynor Hoff. Hoff, born in Nottingham, England learnt his basic stone working skills in his father's masonry yard before serving in the trenches in France during the Great War and later moving to Australia, where he taught sculpture at Sydney Technical College.

Underneath the memorial the basement holds an exhibition of photographs on Australians at War. Entry is through the door outside the memorial on the west side facing the city.

Since 1958 a ceremonial Guard of Honour has been mounted by troops of the Australian Army outside the memorial every Thursday just before 1pm.

Broadway

Continuing on Elizabeth Street turn right under the sandstone railway bridge into Hay Street, turn left into George Street and at Railway Square branch right into *Broadway* following the signpost for Parramatta. Pass an extraordinary example of Victorian Bank architecture on the corner of Regent Street, and Carlton United Breweries, brewers of Fosters Lager, on the left; and the offices of The Sydney Morning Herald and a big Grace Brothers depart ment store on the right. Continue on Broadway to a pedestrian bridge over the road, just past which are some car parking spaces on the left. Some steps near the foot bridge lead into the University Grounds.

Sydney University, designed by Colonial Architect *Edmund Blacket* and built between 1854 – 1860, is like a corner of Oxford uprooted and transported to Australia. With its lush green lawns and cool cloisters it's a haven from the nearby traffic and crowds of the city. Ask if you can go into the stately *Great Hall* adjoining the main quadrangle, with its intricate vaulted wooden roof and beautiful stained glass windows.

Museums

The University is home to two museums. *The Macleay Museum* of Zoology, Anthropology and Photography, on Science Road near the north entrance to the main quadrangle, houses the collection of the Macleay family, donated to the University in 1873. Including specimens gathered by Captain Cook, Charles Darwin and Sir Stamford Raffles, the museum is open 8.30am to 4.30pm Monday to Friday. It isn't very well patronised, so be prepared to search out the caretaker to open the door!

The entrance to the *Nicholson Museum of Antiquities* leads off the south entrance to the main quadrangle. The museum was started in 1860 by Sir Charles Nicholson, with about 100 Greek vases and 400 Egyptian antiquities acquired in Egypt on his way to England in 1856. The collection has been steadily expanded ever since. Opening times are 10.00am to 4.30pm Monday to Friday.

After leaving the University, backtrack along Broadway, drive straight across Railway Square into Pitt Street and turn right at Eddy Avenue past *Central Railway Station*. Central, Sydney's only mainline railway terminus, was built in 1906 on the site of Devonshire Street Cemetery, once the city's main burial ground.

Bondi Beach (previous pages)

Sydney War Memorial (right) in Hyde Park. Local architect Bruce Dellitt intended the design to express with dignity and simplicity the human qualities of courage, endurance and sacrifice. The sculptures surmounting the buttresses on the red granite exterior and the bas-reliefs over the east and west entrances are worth studying. The 120,000 stars in the white marble dome over the hall represent each Australian man and woman who served in the Great War.

Sydney University (above) founded in 1852, on the Great Western Highway just outside the city centre. When the University was completed, the land between it and the city was still devoted to cow pastures. The Great Hall at the university is considered one of the top ten examples of architecture in Australia.

Before construction could start the coffins were dug up and re-interred at Botany Cemetery. The grand clock tower on the north west corner of Central, the tallest clock tower in Sydney, was added some time after the rest of the station was completed.

Entering Elizabeth Street, follow the map to Burton Street and turn right down Forbes Street past the forbidding high sandstone walls of *East Sydney Technical College.* The walls were not built to keep the students in, but rather to hold the prisoners who were inmates of *Darlinghurst Gaol,* Sydney's prison from 1841 until 1914 when the gaol was converted into a technical college.

Victoria Barracks

Turn left at Taylor Square into Oxford Street and find a place to park near Glenmore Road opposite *Victoria Barracks.* The barracks, an immaculate example of Georgian architecture and one of the best preserved colonial barracks in the world, are open to the public every Tuesday at 10.00am, for a changing of the guard ceremony accompanied by music from the Victoria Barracks Band. After the changing of the guard, interesting free tours of the barracks are conducted by ex-servicemen. However the barracks are closed in December and January. Included in the tour is a visit to the army museum in the old military

prison of the barracks, where there are displays of arms, uniforms and memorabilia from the various campaigns the Australian Army has been involved in over the years.

Victoria Barracks was constructed between 1841 and 1848 by *Lieutenant Colonel George Barney* of the Royal Engineers, with the help of 150 French-Canadian convicts transported to Australia following rebellions in Canada in 1837-38, and non-convict stonemasons and carpenters. Built to accommodate a British Regiment of 800 soldiers and their families, the barracks was the base of British garrison regiments in Sydney until the first New South Wales Artillery and Infantry units were

raised in 1870. Although the sandstone for the walls was quarried in Sydney, the slate on the roof of the barracks, the iron columns of the verandahs, the windows, many interior fittings and most of the cedar joinery work was brought from England.

Paddington

Returning to the car, head up Glenmore Road for a short detour around the streets of *Paddington* to see the terraced houses. The whole district has been classified by the National Trust as an example of architecture worthy of preservation. Most of the terraces were built by working class men when the area was sub-divided

Central Station (above). Sydney's first train ran from Redfern Station, at the present site of Railway Square, to Parramatta in September 1855. Central was completed in 1906.

Central Station Clocktower (above). As imposing a clock tower as you will see anywhere.

The former prison chapel (top right) and the entrance gateway to Darlinghurst Gaol (above right), which are now part of East Sydney Technical College. The gaol walls date from 1824, and the entrance gate to the 1870s.

Construction of the enclosing gaol walls was started by Francis Greenway using convict labour, then the gaol was completed to the design of Mortimer Lewis when Greenway was dismissed as colonial architect.

When the gaol was converted into a technical college early this century, the interior cell walls of the cell blocks were demolished and the windows enlarged, but otherwise the general appearance of the gaol has changed very little. A stroll through the grounds will reveal the prison chapel (turned into a library), the Governor's Residence (now the principal's office), the gaol morgue (a switchroom), the gallows yard (a ladies and gents toilet) and the cell blocks (converted into pottery, art and fashion studios and a theatre).

Victoria Barracks (top far right) was built by Lieutenant-Colonel George Barney of the Royal Engineers, who had worked in the West Indies designing fortifications and barracks. The Barracks is one of the longest buildings in Australia, being about as long as the Queen Mary. Some of the detail work in the building is quite interesting, such as the drains from the roof which run inside the verandah pillars, and the cast-iron air vents in the walls, decorated with the Royal Crown.

The Changing of the Guard ceremony at Victoria Barracks (above far right) is followed by a guided tour of the Barracks. (For group tours first ring the barracks on 339 3543). The tour includes a look at Busby's bore, a deep vertical shaft to a tunnel bored through the sandstone for 3.4 kilometres from Lachlan Swamps at the present site of Centennial Park to Hyde Park. The bore, Sydney's first water supply, was started by J. Busby using convict labour, in 1827. Prisoners at the nearby military gaol in the Barracks hauled thousand of gallons of water a day up the shaft using a hand windlass.

and sold off for building in the 1880s and 1890s. Because the lots were bought and built on by individuals rather than developers, there's a tremendous variety of style in the houses, particularly in their white facades decorated in cast iron lacework.

Follow Glenmore Road into Gurner Street and turn right up Cascade Street, that follows the line of old Glenmore Falls, used as a source of water for a gin distillery operating in the area early last century. Pass through Paddington Street and Jersey Road to rejoin Oxford Street.

Head west on Oxford Street following the signs for Bondi. At Bondi Road a long straight hill about five kilometres long runs down to Campbell Parade and *Bondi Beach*. In the old days the trams used to thunder down this hill at great speed, sometimes not even stopping for passengers and giving rise to the expression 'shot through like a Bondi tram'.

Bondi Beach

Along with Waikiki, Brighton, St. Tropez and Malibu; Bondi – pronounced Bon-Dye – ranks among the most famous beaches in the world. Indeed the sea at Bondi is held with the same sort of reverence by many a Sydney surfer as the Ganges is by a Hindu. The beach owes its call to fame by being the closest ocean beach to Sydney, paying a price in summer by attracting crowds of over 25,000 people. It boasts one of Australia's oldest Life Saving Clubs, founded in 1906. If you go for a ritual swim, bathe between the red and yellow flags where the area is patrolled by lifesavers. If walking is more your line, an oceanside track follows the Pacific Ocean for several kilometres from the south end of Bondi Beach to Tamarama and Bronte beaches.

Drive around Bondi Beach on Campbell Parade to Military Road and follow it for four kilometres to Old South Head Road. After about a further kilometre the road passes the majestic, tall, brilliant white *Macquarie Lighthouse*. Permission to visit the lighthouse can be obtained from the Regional Engineer, Department

of Transport by ringing (02) 835 3605. The original lighthouse, which stood on the site from 1816 to 1881, was built by convict Architect *Francis Greenway*.

A short distance further on New South Head Road you pass the hexagonal sided tower of the *Signal Station*, built in the 1840s. The station has been continually manned since January 1790, when Governor Phillip, anxious that the expected Second Fleet might miss the entrance to Sydney Harbour, sent a party of men to the Head to erect a signal flagstaff and keep a fire burning at night. Shipping movements are logged from the tower to this day. In 1858 the first telegraph line in Sydney ran from the Royal Exchange building in Bridge Street to the Signal Station.

Watson's Bay

Where Old South Head Road curves left to begin the descent to Watson's Bay, the green grass of *The Gap Park* marks one of Sydney's more morbid tourist attractions. The 50 metre high cliffs are Sydney's traditional location for suicides. Sydney's worst ever single tragedy occurred here on the night of August 20, 1857, when the migrant ship *Dunbar* was blown onto the rocks below The Gap and all but one of the 122 on board were drowned. Its anchor, recovered in 1907, can be seen mounted in concrete in the park.

Near the road the tiny *St. Peters* *Church of England* designed by *Edmund Blacket* and completed in 1864, was built on the hill with the hope it would be the first building to greet the eyes of passengers arriving in Sydney by ship. According to a brass plaque at the back of the church, the organ, built by Robert and William Grey of London in 1796, once belonged to Napoleon!

Drive down to *Watson's Bay* and park near Military Road next to Robertson Park. Watson's Bay is named after *Robert Watson*, former Quarter Master of the Sirius, the flagship of the First Fleet. After being posted to the Signal Station in 1791, then working as Harbour Master controlling the pilot boats at Watson's Bay, Watson was made the

first Lighthouse Keeper when the Macquarie Lighthouse started operations in 1816 and maintained the light until he died in 1819. Watson's Bay is still the base for pilot boats operating in the harbour.

Doyle's

If it's around lunchtime, consider visiting *Doyle's Restaurant* on the beach at Watson's Bay, Australia's most famous seafood restaurant, owned and operated by the same family for over 100 years. From the tables there's a view right along the length of Sydney Harbour to the city, nine kilometres away. To book, ring Doyle's on 337 2007.

Returning to the car, head north

and follow the one-way system around Watson's Bay to the car park on Cliff Street near the junction with Victoria Street, leave the car and walk to *Camp Cove*. In 1788, when the First Fleet landed at Botany Bay, the settlers found the area swampy and unsuitable for settlement. Governor Phillip set out with three long boats to explore Port Jackson (Sydney Harbour) which Cook had sailed past in the Endeavour in 1770 without stopping to explore. After rounding South Head with his party, Phillip stopped for the night at Camp Cove on January 21, 1788, thus making Camp Cove the first place where white people went ashore in Sydney.

Paddington terraces (above, left and far left) were built as working mens' houses in the 1880s and 1890s. Sydney was just a short tram ride away down Oxford Street. Then the suburb declined, commuters moved to more spacious houses further out from the city and by the end of the Second World War, Paddington had turned into a slum. But since the 1960s it has become fashionable again to live in terraces close to the City and people have moved in and restored them.

Following pages:
Bondi Beach. (left)

Right. An oceanside track follows the cliffs from Bondi (top) to Tamarama Bay and Bronte Beach.

31

33

Shark Beach (right) is a misnomer. There has not been a shark attack in Sydney for over 20 years. Anyway, the beach is protected by a safety net just to make sure.

Shark Beach at Nielson Park (below). The red roof of Greycliffe House, completed in 1852, can be seen in the trees to the right of the beach. Macquarie Lighthouse is in the distance.

Stately Vaucluse House (bottom).

The suburb of Vaucluse (above right) fronting onto Rose Bay is one of Sydney's most sought after residential addresses.

The austere looking estate (above far right) is a girls' convent. New South Head Road is to the rear.

Previous pages:

Camp Cove (above left), the first landing place of white settlers in Sydney harbour.

Doyles Restaurant, Watsons Bay (above centre), Australia's best known seafood restaurant, run by the same family for over 100 years.

South Head (above right). Lady Bay nudist beach is on the right.

St. Peter's Church of England (below), purported to contain a church organ that once belonged to Napoleon.

South Head

From Camp Cove a 40 minute return walk leads to *South Head*. At the north end of the cove walk up the wooden steps to an old road paved with sandstone slabs and follow it to a gun emplacement containing a sizeable cannon on an iron carriage manufactured by W.G. Armstrong & Co. Newcastle on Tyne in 1872. Keep to the path on top of the rocks, past *Lady Bay*, one of Sydney's two official nudist beaches, to reach South Head after a further 10 minutes walk. At the tip of the Head stands the red and white striped *Hornby Lighthouse*, completed in 1858 after the tragedy of the Dunbar. The lighthouse was named after Sir Phipps Hornby, Commander In Chief of the British Pacific Fleet. Scattered about the head are old fortifications dating from the 1870s to the Second World War.

Vaucluse House

Backtrack to the car and take Hopetoun Avenue out of Watson's Bay. Turn right down Fitzwilliam Road past Parsley Bay into Wentworth Road and after a few hundred metres, turn left up the drive and into the carpark in the grounds of *Vaucluse House.*

Vaucluse House received its name from the 'Gentleman Convict', Sir Henry Brown Hayes, who is thought to have named it after Fontaine-de-Vaucluse in France, where an underground stream emerges into a steep sided valley in a setting not dissimilar to that of Vaucluse in Sydney. Hayes, an Irish Baronet, was transported for abducting a Quaker heiress and forcing her to marry him. He bought Vaucluse and 100 surrounding acres for 100 pounds in 1803 and built a stone cottage there. Being frightened of snakes, Hayes imported barrels full of Irish soil which was dug into a trench around his house by a gang of convicts. The walls of Hayes' 1803 house comprise the walls of the living room in the present home, making Vaucluse House in part at least, the oldest house in Sydney.

These days Vaucluse House is substantially the same as it was in about 1840, when it was rebuilt to suit the taste of *William Charles Wentworth* who bought the house in 1827 from Captain John Piper. W.C. Wentworth was fathered from a union between D'Arcy Wentworth, an Assistant Surgeon travelling out to Australia with the Second Fleet and Catherine Crawley, a convict woman transported for stealing clothes, travelling on the same ship. William Charles went on to become one of the 'greats' of Sydney's early colonial days as an explorer, author, barrister and statesman. Read all about this remarkable man in the museum at the house.

From Vaucluse House it's a short walk or drive along Wentworth Road and Greycliffe Avenue to a sheltered harbour swimming beach at *Nielson Park*. Nearby *Greycliffe House*, completed in 1852, was once part of the Wentworth estate.

A Sydney Harbour ferry, the 'Greycliffe', was involved in Sydney's worst ferry disaster. Travelling from Circular Quay to Watson's Bay at 4.15pm on November 3, 1927, the Greycliffe was sliced in two by the liner 'Tahiti'. Forty two people were drowned including seven children on their way home from school.

Returning to the car, join Vaucluse Road passing the *Convent of the Sacred Heart* (1884) looming over the tranquil waters of Rose Bay like Colditz Castle, and turn right onto New South Head Road, the main road back to Sydney.

Tonight, consider trying the Summit Restaurant on top of Australia Square, off George Street. On the 47th level, the restaurant is the largest tower-top revolving restaurant in the world and takes $1\frac{3}{4}$ hours to revolve the full circle. A pianist plays Monday to Saturday and there is a small dance floor. Free parking is available in the basement off George Street. The cuisine is international with the emphasis on fresh local seafood or there is a choice of buffet luncheon or dinner.

WEDNESDAY

Colonial heritage and a trip by ferry

The first part of today's tour, a stroll up Macquarie Street, stopping
at places of interest on the way, is a tribute to Governor Macquarie and his
convict Architect Francis Greenway. Then the rest of the day is taken up
with a trip to Manly.

Governor Macquarie

Following the struggle to found the colony under *Governor Phillip* (1788 – 1792), fresh development was stifled in the first years of the 19th century through the influence of the New South Wales Corps or 'Rum Corps' as they were known, who were able to control the finances of Sydney by using Bengal Rum as a means of exchange, as there was a great scarcity of hard currency. An attempt to put the colony's affairs in order when *Governor Bligh* (of Mutiny on the Bounty fame) was sent out as Governor, ended in disaster in 1808 when the Rum Corps rose and deposed him. So when Brigadier General *Lachlan Macquarie* arrived in 1810 with his own regiment of Royal Highlanders, though he was able to break the control of the Rum Corps, the administration of Sydney was in a mess or as Macquarie put it:

'... I found the colony barely emerging from infantile imbecility and suffering from various privations and disabilities; the country impenetrable beyond 40 miles from Sydney; agriculture in a yet languishing state; commerce in its early dawn; revenue unknown; threatened by famine; distracted by faction; the public buildings in a state of dilapidation and mouldering to decay; the few roads and bridges formerly constructed, rendered almost impassable; the population depressed by poverty; no public credit nor private confidence; the morals of the great mass of the population in the lowest state of debasement and religious worship almost totally neglected.'.

During his 12 year term as Viceroy, ending in 1822, Macquarie certainly transformed Sydney from a state of 'infantile imbecility' into a more respectable colony. His achievements included the erection of over 200 public buildings and the granting of land for Sydney's two cathedrals, setting aside Hyde Park as a public park (1810) and founding the Botanical Gardens (1816), making the colony's first coinage (1813) and opening its first bank, the Bank of New South Wales (1817), promoting the first crossing of the Blue Mountains (1813) and founding the new settlements of Richmond, Windsor and Liverpool, on the plains around Sydney. Macquarie could upset people by his autocratic and arrogant style of leadership and his insufferable vanity – he named Macquarie Street after himself and Elizabeth Street after his wife, but there's no diminishing the work he did as Governor.

Macquarie hardly need have concerned himself about his name being carried forward for posterity; today in Sydney there are four Macquarie Avenues, three Macquarie Places, nine Macquarie Roads, 17 Macquarie Streets, one Macquarie Drive, one Macquarie Grove, one Macquarie Terrace, one Macquarie University and one Macquarie Shopping Centre.

From Circular Quay walk up Phillip Street and turn left at Bridge Street. If you've left without your breakfast go into the Inter-Continental Hotel on the corner of Phillip and Bridge Streets and have a coffee in the cocktail lounge in the courtyard of the old Treasury (1849) which has been incorporated into the hotel. The first shipments from the Australian gold fields were stored in the Treasury. The Colonial Secretary's Building occupies the corner on the other side of Bridge Street.

The Conservatorium of Music

Continue on Bridge Street past the statue of Edward VII on horseback to the castellated *Conservatorium of Music*. Free instrument recitals are given by students in the Conservatorium's Concert Hall during term time, check the times given on the noticeboard at the entrance. The Conservatorium was originally the stables for Government House.

Designed by Francis Greenway, an Architect transported to Australia in 1814, for forging a signature on a building contract, who was appointed Civil Architect by Macquarie in 1816, the stables were intended for a palatial Government House that was never built. Commissioner J.T. Bigge, who arrived in Sydney in 1819 to conduct an enquiry into the affairs of the colony, stopped the building of Government House because the design was too costly and criticised Macquarie for making the stables 'such a palace for horses'. To passengers arriving in Sydney at the time, the stables were the biggest building on the horizon and they thought they were looking at Government House.

The Garden Palace

With the entrance to the Conservatorium of Music at your back, turn left, walk up the grass verge and go through the gate of the *Royal Botanic Gardens*, then turn right and follow the path. Where you are walking was the site of the Garden Palace, a splendid edifice built for an International Exhibition in 1879. The Palace, the biggest structure completed in Sydney up to that time, stretched from the Conservatorium of Music to the present site of the

State Library of New South Wales. With a dome 64 metres high and a hall 244 metres long, it was longer and higher than the Queen Victoria Building in the city. The Palace burnt to the ground in 1882 only three years after it was completed. Sydney's first steam trams carried visitors to the Exhibition from Redfern Station to Macquarie Street in 1879.

As you are walking through the gardens look to the right over the fence to the art-deco styled cream tiled facade of British Medical

Macquarie Street (above) and the western extremity of the Royal Botanic Gardens.

A narrow neck of sand (previous pages) now engulfed by development, joins the suburb of Fairlight (foreground) to North Head.

Association House (1929) at 135 – 137 Macquarie Street. Koalas and knights holding shields are mounted on the top of the buttresses.

The State Library

Pass a statue of Governor Phillip by the Italian sculptor Simonetti, unveiled during Victoria's Diamond Jubilee Celebration in 1897 and cross Shakespeare Place to the *State Library of New South Wales*. Before leaving the gardens a short detour to the left takes you through the Pioneers Garden to the tropical plant displays in the Pyramid Glasshouse.

The State Library, Australia's oldest library founded in 1826, contains an excellent reference library and the *Mitchell and Dixon collections*, between them the greatest collection of Australiana in the world. The Mitchell Library contains such priceless items as Cook's diaries, the log from HMS Bounty and eight out of the 10 existing journals written by members of the First Fleet (available

The Pyramid Glasshouse (top left) in the Royal Botanic Gardens contains a collection of tropical plants. On a hot summer's day the Glasshouse is like a Turkish bath inside.

Governor Macquarie's 'Palace for Horses' (above left) was once the stables for Government House. When the motor car came along and made the stables redundant, they were converted into a Conservatorium of Music.

Governor Phillip's statue (above), unveiled during Queen Victoria's Diamond Jubilee celebrations, reflects the mood of that era.

The Pioneer Garden (left) in the Royal Botanic Gardens.

for viewing on micro-film). Many of these treasures were donated in 1907 when David Scott Mitchell gave his entire collection of 60,000 articles of Australiana to the state. Sir William Dixon, who started collecting when David Scott Mitchell finished, donated his own collection of 20,000 items of Australiana when he died in 1952. Covering most of the floor space in the lobby of the State Library is an intricately crafted representation of Abel Tasman's map of Australia in marble and brass. Leave the State Library by the main entrance, descend the steps and turn left.

Parliament House

Continue south on Macquarie Street, past the new State Library building, opened in 1988, to *New South Wales Parliament House*. The Georgian style double-storey verandahed building was built in 1811 – 1816 as the north wing to the 'Rum Hospital' and converted for use by the State Legislative Council in 1829. It is the oldest Parliament in Australia. The 'Rum Hospital' received its name because in 1811 when Macquarie entrusted a triumvirate with the building of a new hospital, he paid them by granting them a monopoly on the import of rum into the Colony for three years.

Parliament House is open from 9.00am to 5.00pm on weekdays only. Members of the public are free to walk through the designated areas. Make sure you pick up an interesting little free booklet about Parliament House from the desk at the entrance.

Around the walls of the exhibition area towards the back of Parliament House, are two permanent photography displays, one in colour by David Moore on the Australian flora and landscape, and the other in black and white by Max Dupain of New South Wales' colonial period public works. In the Parliament House Library there is an illustrated history of the discovery and settlement of Sydney and the story of the New South Wales Parliament. Displayed in a glass case are the opal encrusted gold scissors that were

officially, and I stress the word officially, used to open the Harbour Bridge in 1932.

When Parliament is sitting, the action can be watched from the public galleries of the Upper House *(Legislative Council)* and Lower House *(Legislative Assembly)*. When it is not sitting, which is most of the time, the public are free to go into the respective chambers. The shell of the Legislative Council Chamber is a pre-fabricated iron structure, that was originally sent to Australia from England to be used as a church in the goldfields. Due to a shortage of housing in Melbourne at the time, it was used for accommodation there before being bought by the New South Wales Government, dismantled and freighted to Sydney, then re-erected for the new Council Chamber.

Sydney Hospital

Sydney Hospital, next to Parliament House, occupies the ground where the central wing of the Rum Hospital once stood, demolished in 1885 to make way for the present structure. Behind the main building the *Florence Nightingale Wing*, opened in 1869 to receive nurses trained by Florence Nightingale, is the oldest part of the hospital.

Outside the hospital on Macquarie Street, the statue of Fiaschi the bronze wild boar was donated by a family in Florence whose relatives had worked as Surgeons at the hospital. Patients rub its nose for good luck as they enter the hospital. As you walk past, toss a dollar coin into the wishing fountain beneath the boar to help the hospital. No doubt patients entering the hospital these days stand a much better chance of recovery than in the days of the Rum Hospital, when the patients were locked up at night with convict nurses and warders.

The Mint Museum

Next on the agenda on Macquarie Street, the *Mint Museum* occupying the old south wing of the Rum Hospital, contains a *Museum of Colonial Decorative Art*. Numismatic and

Take away the steeple from St James Church (above far left) and the building looks like the courthouse as originally designed. St James (1822) is the oldest church in the City of Sydney. A flight of steps next to the church leads to St James underground station.

New South Wales Parliament House (above centre) Australia's oldest parliament. The State Legislative Council Chamber on the right is a pre-fabricated structure with a framework of iron that was made in England, transported to Melbourne where it was used for housing, before being re-crated and moved to Sydney.

The State Library of New South Wales (above) contains, among many other things, the Mitchell and Dixon collections, the biggest collection of Australiana in the world.

The Mint Museum (far left), was the south wing of Macquarie's 'Rum Hospital' before conversion into Australia's first mint.

Francis Greenway, an emancipated convict transported for forging a signature on a building contract, designed St James Church and Hyde Park Convict Barracks (left).

Manly hydrofoil on Sydney Harbour (above).

If you travel to Manly by hydrofoil (right) try to find a seat outside. The view is so much better than if you are crammed below decks with the commuters engrossed in their newspapers.

philatelic collections and examples of some of the first Australian made furniture, clocks, musical instruments, pottery and silver are displayed. From a historical point of view, one of the most interesting coins on display is the 'Holey Dollar'. Because of the shortage of legal tender in Sydney when Macquarie arrived, he bought 10,000 Spanish dollars and had William Hershell, a transported forger, punch a circular section from each coin. The round dump was counterstamped 'New South Wales 1813' on the obverse and 'Fifteen Pence' on the reverse, while the remaining Holey Dollar was stamped 'Five Shillings'. Forty thousand holey dollars were issued and remained in circulation in Sydney until 1829. The Mint Museum is open seven days a week 10.00am to 5.00pm except Wednesdays 12 noon to 5.00pm.

Hyde Park Convict Barracks

On the corner of Macquarie Street and Prince Alfred Road stands *Hyde Park Barracks Museum.* During the early years of the colony, convicts labouring on public works were fed and clothed but not housed and either slept rough or begged for a place to sleep at night. With hundreds of convicts wandering the streets of Sydney every evening after work, crime was rampant. Macquarie had Francis Greenway design and build Hyde Park Convict Barracks (1817 – 1819), a three storey brick and sandstone dormitory to sleep 800 convicts. Opened on June 4, 1819 by Macquarie, the first 589 convicts staying in the barracks were served that night 'a most excellent dinner, plum pudding and an allowance of punch'.

When transportation ended the barracks was a hostel for single

immigrant women, then a home for old and destitute women and finally offices for Government departments, before it was restored and re-opened in 1984 as a *Museum of Social History in New South Wales.* The most interesting part of the museum is on the top floor; one room has an exhibition on Macquarie's Sydney and Greenway's buildings and another has been recreated as a convict dormitory with rough hewn timber stanchions supporting rows of canvas hammocks. Put your feet up for five minutes, swing on a hammock and listen to the tape recording about living conditions for convicts in the barracks. The barracks are open seven days a week, 10.00am to 5.00pm except Tuesday from 12 noon to 5.00pm.

St. James Church

Cross Macquarie Street to St. James Church (1819 – 1822), directly opposite the barracks. St. James was designed originally as a courtroom by Francis Greenway, then Macquarie asked Greenway to change his plans to turn it into a church. Inside the church the fine craftsmanship of the polished marble railing and mosaic floor of the sanctuary make a striking contrast to the relative plainness of the rest of the interior.

Francis Greenway's *Supreme Court building,* directly behind the church, still functions as a sheriff's office and has four working courts. A door outside St. James Church on the west side of the steeple facing the Supreme Court, leads to the brick vaulted church crypt, possibly intended to be used as cells if the church had fulfilled its original function as a court. One of the chambers in the crypt, contains a children's chapel with frescoes of scenes from the bible transposed to Australian settings.

The Supreme Court

On the same side of Macquarie Street next to St. James Church, is the modern New South Wales Supreme Court building, containing about 40 courts including arbitration courts, federal courts and supreme courts. Its showpiece, the

amphitheatred Bronco Court, on the 13th level, can be viewed from the press gallery when the court is in session. One floor further up at the top of the building, the Law Courts' Restaurant is open to the public. The coffee lounge, open from 7.00am to 3.30pm, serves breakfast and snacks and the restaurant, open 11.30am to 2.00pm serves exceptionally cheap meals with no charge for the fantastic view of Hyde Park, Macquarie Street and the Botanical Gardens.

On the forecourt in front of St. James Church near Macquarie Street, go down the steps leading to St. James underground station and catch a train one stop to *Circular Quay.* While you are waiting for your train at St. James you will have time to admire the splendour of the station's original 1920's colour scheme of cream and green tiles.

Circular Quay

At Circular Quay pick up a free copy of the timetable of Sydney ferries and hydrofoils with connecting buses, from one of the ticket counters. Ferries to Manly run about every half an hour and hydrofoils about every 20 minutes.

One of the Manly Ferries (left). Ferries have been part of everyday life in Sydney since the earliest days of the colony, when a punt ran from Sydney Cove to Parramatta. These days, over 10,000 people a day commute to work on ferries. Sydney has the second busiest network of ferries in the world after Hong Kong.

Balmoral Beach on Middle Harbour (above).

Manly Cove Beach (right).

Usually, the Ferry stops at the Wharf. But at 9 a.m. on 10th March, 1983 (below) the recently launched ferry 'Freshwater' was berthing at Manly Wharf, when the ship's computer engaged the propellor, sending the ship through the swimming enclosure net and on to Manly Cove Beach. The 'Freshwater' was refloated on the high tide at 3 p.m . with the help of a tug.

The 1903 Manly Horse Tram (bottom) once ran on rails around Manly.

The start of a windsurfing race at Manly Cove (above right).

The Corso (below right) dates from the 1850s when Henry Gilbert Smith cleared the bush between Manly Wharf and the Ocean Beach, a distance of 500 metres. Smith called his new street 'The Corso', after a street in Rome.

The Manly Ferry arrives at the wharf on Manly Cove (previous pages). Little Manly Cove is on the right.

Wednesday

Manly Ocean Beach (above). The first Norfolk Island Pines were planted by Henry Gilbert Smith. Norfolk Island, 1500 miles north east of Sydney, discovered by Captain Cook, was colonised two and a half weeks after Sydney by members of the First Fleet because the tall pine trees growing there were thought to be ideal for ship's masts.

Manly Ocean Beach (previous pages). Sydney Harbour lies beyond, and the skyscrapers of the city, about 10 kilometres distant, can be picked out on the right.

Ferries are to Sydney what gondolas are to Venice, they are part of everyday life and thousands of people commute to work on them daily. While you are on your way out to Manly, bear in mind the motto of the Port Jackson Steam Ship Company formed in 1881, that ran the Manly Ferries 'Four pence spent on a trip to Manly is better than a pound on medicine'. Hydrofoils to Manly leave from No. 2 Jetty Circular Quay, fares $4.00 for adults and children, ferries to Manly leave from No. 3 Jetty, fares $3.00 for adults and $1.50 for children.

Manly

After entering Sydney Harbour on

January 21, 1788 and spending the night at Camp Cove, Phillip's longboats started exploring the harbour shoreline the following morning. According to Phillip's dispatches to England, on January 22, 1788:

'The boats in passing near a point of land in the harbour were seen by a number of men and 20 of them waded into the water unarmed, received what was offered to them and examined the boats with a curiosity that gave me a much higher opinion of them .... and their confidence and manly bearing made me give the name Manly Cove to this place'.

The following day Phillip went on to

discover and name Sydney Cove.

Manly remained an area of sparsely populated bushland until the 1850s, when *Henry Gilbert Smith,* inspired by Brighton from his native Sussex in England, developed 120 acres of land he owned in Manly. Smith erected a ferry wharf at Manly Cove, built a hotel nearby and cleared the bush from the wharf through to the ocean beach 500 metres away, to form a road he called *'The Corso'* after a street in Rome. With tents where refreshments were served, a public bathhouse, maze, gardens, swings, walks and a ferry service to bring day-trippers from Sydney, Smith had turned Manly into a resort 60 years before Bondi

became popular.

Strange as it may seem, public bathing was banned at this time in Manly in view of a public place, between 6.00am and 8.00pm. William Gocher, the Editor of the Manly and North Shore News, announced in his paper in October 1902 that he would bathe in daylight hours and damn the consequences. Gocher was arrested, but a local Magistrate wouldn't fine him and following further campaigning the law was repealed in November 1903. That year the Sly brothers started Australia's first Life Saving Service at Manly, operating from an old fishing boat and Sydney's beach and swimming tradition was born.

The annual Surf Carnival at Manly (above). The sand of Shelley Beach in the background is made up from a mixture of finely ground shells.

There's plenty to do in Manly. A good start would be to walk through The Corso opposite *Manly Wharf to Manly Tourist Promotions* on the promenade, to pick up a free map of Manly with locations of places of interest and a shopping guide.

Walks

Easy walks following oceanside and harbourside tracks lead to parks, bushland and beaches. From the ferry wharf turn left along West Esplanade past *Manly Museum* and *Marineland* to a waterside path that follows the harbour foreshore past *Fairlight Beach* to a park at North Harbour. Or, turn right at the Ferry Wharf along East Esplanade to Stuart Street, walk the length of Stuart Street past *Little Manly Cove* and turn left at the end to follow a foreshore track leading, after about five minutes walk, to *Spring Cove Beach* surrounded by natural bushland. On September 7, 1790, Governor Phillip was speared through the shoulder by an aborigine when he stepped ashore at Spring Cove, searching for an aborigine who had been captured earlier at Manly, held at Sydney and later escaped. Phillip, who insisted that his men were not to retaliate, made a full recovery after six weeks rest.

From Manly Wharf a bus service runs four kilometres to *North Head Lookout* on top of the cliffs at the north entrance to Sydney Harbour. On the way the bus passes the entrance to the *Quarantine Station*. Immigrant ships entering Sydney carrying passengers infected by contagious diseases, stopped at the Quarantine Station for six weeks while all passengers and crew went through quarantine procedures. The station is administered by the National Parks and Wildlife Service and to go on one of their guided tours you need to book in advance by ringing 977 6229.

From the south end of Manly Ocean Beach, a 20 minute walk on

Marine Parade leads to *Shelley Beach*. With a view looking back onto Manly Beach, Shelley Beach is the only west facing beach on the east coast of Australia.

A useful alternative to a walk or a tour, particularly if it's a hot day, is to find a patch of sand and simply relax on the beach for a few hours. That should be enough to work up a thirst ready for quenching in one of the bars on The Corso or in the Manly Pacific Park Royal Hotel.

Tonight, why not leaf through your brochure from Manly Tourist Promotions to choose a restaurant for your evening meal, before taking the Manly Ferry back to Circular Quay. The choice of restaurants in Manly covers the gamut of international cuisine, with prices to suit all pockets from the five star Manly Pacific Park Royal to backstreet take-aways. For excellent seafood and relaxing water views, Le Kiosk at Shelly Beach (977 4122) or the Manly Pier Seafood Restaurant on Commonwealth Parade (949 2677) are both upmarket, but good.

The quiet cloisters and chapel of St Patricks Seminary (above) are open to the public once a year in January on Colonial Day. Basking proudly in the sunshine on the hill above Manly Beach, modelled on Maynooth Seminary in Ireland.

North Head and the entrance to Sydney Harbour (above right) from Watsons Bay. Just for the record, North and South Head are separated by 1500 metres of water, the Sydney Harbour shoreline including the Parramatta and Lane Cove Rivers is 250 kilometres long and encloses 55 square kilometres of water.

The cliffs at North Head (right). Chris Bonnington likes to climb them when he is in Sydney.

57

THURSDAY

Sydney bushland and the Northern Beaches

Following a stroll in the morning taking in some of the last and grandest
buildings of the colonial period built in Sydney, then a drive to the sprawling
Ku-ring-gai Chase National Park, 50 kilometres to the north, we finish
the day with a visit in the evening to the bars and nightclubs of the
Leicester Square of Sydney, Kings Cross.

Colonial Architecture

From Circular Quay, walk along Loftus Street passing the *Customs House* on the corner, designed by colonial Architect James Barnet. Completed in 1885, the Customs House has the names on scrolls of various outposts of the British Empire decorating the facade. Continue on Loftus Street to Macquarie Place, a location that if anywhere could enjoy the title of 'the Cradle of Australian Civilisation', this would surely be it.

The small park at *Macquarie Place* was set aside by Governor Macquarie from part of the garden of Old Government House. It is thought to have been close to the spot where early in the morning of January 26, 1788, 26 officers and marines first stepped ashore at Sydney Cove from the First Fleet, raised the Union Jack, fired four volleys of small arms and drank a toast to the new colony. A portable canvas structure carried on one of the ships and erected nearby, was the first Governor's House. The flagship of the First Fleet, an old frigate that had served in the American War of Independence and was renamed the Sirius for its new mission after the brightest star in the southern sky, sank off Norfolk Island in March 1790 while on a journey to China for

supplies. The anchor from the Sirius and one of its cannons recovered in 1907, can be found in the park. A sandstone obelisk nearby, designed by Francis Greenway and erected in 1818, is the benchmark for road distances from Sydney to the rest of Australia.

Continuing on Loftus Street between the grand sandstone buildings of the *Lands' Department* on the right, built over a period of 20 years from the 1870s to the 1890s, and the *Education Department* building on the left, completed 1913, turn left at Bent Street. The street's irregular course once skirted the vegetable garden of Old Government House. Turn right at Bligh Street, glancing back down Bent Street to see the stately onion domed clock tower of the Lands' Department building. Forty eight niches in the outside walls of the Lands' Department building contain some statues of Australian explorers and legislators. Twenty five niches were left unfilled when the building was completed, and they have remained vacant ever since.

Circular Quay at dusk (previous pages).

Sir Thomas Mitchell explorer (left) one of the prominent figures from early New South Wales colonial days who's statues decorate the facade of the Lands Department Building on Bridge Street. A wooden bridge, erected October 1788 (the first in the colony) and replaced by a stone bridge 1803-4, stood near the corner of Bridge and Pitt Streets.

Circular Quay and the City (below left).

Macquarie Place (below), packed with office workers eating their lunch on weekdays, is deserted at the same time on a Saturday. The anchor and a cannon from the 'Sirius', flagship of the First Fleet, are on the right. Francis Greenway's obelisk to mark road distances in New South Wales, erected 1818, is on the left near the steps. Sydney's first streetlight, burning whale oil, was erected in the park in 1826. The original facade and marble bar of the Customs House Hotel on the north-west side of Macquarie Place, have been incorporated into the Ramada Renaissance Hotel.

Above. The Cenotaph, Martin Place, on 11th November, 1986.

The tower overlooking Darling Harbour Docks (above right) logs all shipping movements in and out of Sydney.

Bligh Street is named after the hapless *Governor Bligh*, who, following the Mutiny on the Bounty enjoyed a short term as Governor of N.S.W. before being deposed by a mutiny on land during the Sydney Rum Rebellion of 1808. Walk past the back entrance of the Wentworth Hotel on Bligh Street and turn left at Hunter Street. The *N.S.W. Government Information Centre* on the ground floor of the Goodsell Building on the corner of Hunter and Phillip Street, sells books, maps and posters and provides free general information about the State of N.S.W. The Centre is open 8.45am to 4.45pm Monday to Friday. *The N.S.W. Government Travel Centre* is just a few minutes walk from here at the corner of Pitt Street and Spring Street.

Martin Place

Continue on Phillip Street and turn right to enter Martin Place pedestrian mall. At the Half Tix Kiosk on the left near Elizabeth Street, half price tickets to Sydney shows and concerts are available on the day of purchase, between noon and 6pm. Free tourist information and maps are available in the adjoining Sydney Convention and Visitors' Bureau Kiosk.

Heading west down the pedestrian mall; at the amphi-theatre in the centre, lunchtime crowds enjoy free shows ranging from sheep shearing

displays to ethnic dance groups and live rock bands. Pass the *Dobell Memorial Sculpture*, (1979), an erection of stainless steel pyramids one on top of the other known locally as the 'Silver Shish Kebab' and cross Pitt Street to *James Barnet's G.P.O. building*.

When construction of the G.P.O. was commenced in 1866, Australia's postal services had advanced remarkably since the appointment of Australia's first postmaster in 1809. That year Isaac Nichols Esquire; transported for stealing a donkey, started a post office at his own home. The G.P.O. was completed in stages and opened for the colony's centenary in 1887, though the clock wasn't fitted to the clocktower until 1891. In 1942 the Sydney Council, concerned that the 64 metre high G.P.O. clocktower may be used as a reference point by Japanese pilots to bomb the centre of Sydney, dismantled the tower and put the pieces in storage. The tower stayed down for over 20 years until it was dusted off and re-erected in 1963.

In Martin Place opposite the G.P.O., stands the *Cenotaph* where a dawn service is held every ANZAC Day and a memorial service every Remembrance Day at 11am on November 11th. Stop for a while to ponder the message 'LEST WE FORGET', inscribed on the side of the Cenotaph. Australia suffered tremendous losses in both wars, and casualties in the Malayan

Emergency and Vietnam. A memorial service played by members of the Victoria Barracks Brass Band takes place at the Cenotaph every Thursday at 12.30pm.

George Street

At the junction of Martin Place and George Street, several banks and insurance companies have their offices. Constructed at the turn of the century and early this century, the buildings are styled in typical 'solid as a rock' fashion of the period, with polished marble and granite predominating. On a wet Sydney winter's day, when commuters with umbrellas raised are hurrying between rain squalls, squint your eyes and try to tell yourself that

Above. Glebe Island Container Terminal, left, and Glebe Island swing bridge, lower right, in the docks. During the Second World War Glebe Island was the disembarking point for American troops arriving in Sydney. On 28th March 1942 the first 8,000 American troops to arrive in Sydney were carried from the Queen Mary to Glebe Island by harbour ferries.

The view of Barrenjoey Headland (top), from Commodore Heights at West Head.

West Head Road (above left) in Ku-ring-gai Chase National Park, 14,712 hectares of bushland on the north east outskirts of Sydney. Planners set aside the area, only 24 km north of Sydney, in 1894. The sandstone plateau of the park, dissected by scenic waterways, is well known for its Aboriginal carvings, wild flowers, bush walks and picnic areas.

Gladesville Bridge (left).

McCarr's Creek Road (above) winds through unspoilt bush.

Thursday

Tame kookaburras at West Head (below left).

Houses on Church Point at Pittwater (below right).

Warriewood Beach (bottom).

you're not in the City of London.

Turning right down *George Street;* the High Street of Governor Phillip's Sydney renamed George Street by Governor Macquarie after George III, pass *Australia Square Tower* on the right. Good views of Sydney can be enjoyed from the revolving *Summit Restaurant* at the top. A short distance later, pass the *Qantas Centre* office tower on the left. In the foyer of the entrance to the tower off Jamison Street, standing on pedestals on the carpet are some of the engines that have seen service in Qantas aircraft since shortly after the First World War. Qantas is the world's second oldest airline.

A little further along George Street at the junction of Essex Street, is the site of Sydney's first gaol. Public hangings here were a popular entertainment of the day. A plaque on the Regent Hotel, at the corner of Essex Street and Harrington Street, cheerfully announces 'The First Execution. Thomas Barrett, a First Fleet convict was hanged near this place on February 27, 1788 for stealing provisions and was buried nearby.'. On a less sombre note, the café in the *Regent Hotel* is an excellent place to rest your feet and enjoy a coffee and a bite to eat.

Last but not least; continuing on George Street and under the Cahill

Harbord Beach (left) with St Patrick's Seminary at Manly in the distance. At Harbord Beach on January 15th 1915, Duke Kahanamoku, a Hawaiian-born world champion swimmer, built his own board and gave Australia its first exhibition of surf board riding.

Curl Curl Beach (below).

Dee Why Beach (bottom right).

Bottom Left. Turimetta Beach in the foreground, with the 5 kilometre stretch of Narrabeen and Collaroy Beach behind. The sea off Long Reef (middle distance top left) is the last resting place of some of Sydney's old ferries, scuttled in 25 fathoms of water close to the shore.

67

Expressway, a minute or so's walk brings you to James Barnet's *Rocks Police Station* (1882). Note the lion holding a baton in its mouth on the keystone above the entrance. The police station is built on the site of the First Fleet Hospital, a crude structure thrown together from branches, bark and wattle, to house the sick when the First Fleet landed.

The Docks

Assuming you have managed to beg, borrow or steal a car, continue in motorised fashion in a northerly direction on George Street and turn right into *Hickson Road*. In 1900, 113 people died of the plague in Sydney, mostly in The Rocks. Rats from ships at nearby Walsh Bay had

spread the disease and the Sydney Harbour Trust was formed in 1901 to clear up The Rocks and prevent another outbreak occurring. The Trust resumed ownership of private wharves running from Walsh Bay to Darling Harbour, quarantined the area and the Trust's first President, Robert Hickson, demolished houses and ware-houses to build a 30 metre

wide road around the waterfront, enclosed on the landward side by a high rat proof wall. In a bacteriological laboratory set up on nearby Goat Island, Dr. Frank Tidswell proved by experimenting (for the first time) that it was the fleas carried by rats, that spread bubonic plague.

Follow Hickson Road under the Harbour Bridge and past Pier One.

The Spit Bridge at Middle Harbour (left) receives its name because of the sandspit on the south side of the bridge. For 38 years, from 1850 to 1888, a man called Ellery worked the crossing with a hand punt. Many Sydney residents can still remember when the crossing was serviced by a cable ferry before the first bridge was built in 1924. The present Spit Bridge with a single lift span dates from 1959. At Clontarf Park behind the beach on the left of the picture, an Irishman, H. J. O'Farrell shot and wounded Prince Alfred, Duke of Edinburgh, son of Queen Victoria in 1868 while he was having a picnic there. O'Farrell was hanged for his trouble.

Long traffic queues form when the Spit Bridge (top) lifts several times a day to allow yachts and ferries to pass.

Boronia House 1885 (above) on Military Road Mosman, for many years the local library, is now a restaurant.

Pier 4, houses the Wharf Theatre and Restaurant. The Theatre, opened in 1984, is currently leased by the Sydney Theatre Company. There are conducted tours which give a history of the wharf and theatre and take visitors back stage and to the rehearsal rooms. To book tours and find out what is currently showing, ring 250 1700. Continue past Darling Harbour docks into Sussex Street and turn right at the lights at Market Street to join the Western Distributor. Cross the Glebe Island swing bridge (1901), then after a further two kilometres turn right onto Victoria Road.

Glebe Island, these days joined to the suburb of Rozelle by land recla-

mations, was the site of the Sydney abattoirs from 1852 to early this century. These days the island is host to massive grain handling silos and a busy container ship terminal.

Passing through the suburbs of Rozelle and Drummoyne, crossing Iron Cove Bridge (1954) and negotiating 13 sets of traffic lights on the way, go up and over the graceful arch of *Gladesville Bridge.* The bridge's 305 metre span was the longest concrete arch span in the world when it was completed in October 1964. The Gladesville Bridge replaced an old swing bridge opened in February 1881, which was the first bridge spanning the main channel of Sydney Harbour. The swing bridge in

William Street (far left) with the Hyatt Kingsgate Hotel at the top.

The illuminated Coca-Cola sign on Darlinghurst Road at Kings Cross (below far left).

Trains are usually the last thing on the minds of visitors to Kings Cross (bottom far left).

'Les Girls' all male revue (left) has been going for over 25 years.

The 'world famous' Pink Pussycat (below left). Say no more.

The El Alamein Fountain Kings Cross (below) commemorates the men of the Australian Ninth Division who fought in North Africa during the Second World War.

turn replaced the so-called Bedlam Ferry, crossing the Parramatta River two kilometres to the west at the Great North Road. The ferry received its name because of the nearby location of Gladesville Mental Hospital. In fact the point on the north shore of the river from where the ferries used to leave has been called Bedlam Point ever since.

Houses at Hunters Hill

As the road forks coming down from Gladesville Bridge, take the right fork signposted for Lane Cove, then a short distance later turn off the highway following the signposts for Hunters Hill. Follow Church Street, Alexandra Street and Woolwich Road to Clarke Reserve, a grassy park on the water-front at Clarke's Point with good views of the harbour. The Woolwich Pier Hotel (1892) at the end of Woolwich Road; with its bar and bistro, a good spot to stop for a bite of lunch, enjoys a view straight down the harbour to the Harbour Bridge from the first floor.

The picturesque, charming suburb of Hunters Hill owes its existence to the French brothers Didier and Jules Joubert, who emigrated to Sydney in the 1840s, bought 200 acres of land at Hunters Hill, subdivided it and with 40 stonemasons they brought out from Italy, built elegant homes from locally quarried sandstone. The suburb has changed very little since the houses were finished, most of the 200 or so homes built by the Joubert brothers are still standing.

Ku-ring-gai Chase

Backtrack through Hunters Hill to rejoin the main road, follow Burns Bay Road and Centennial Avenue to Epping Road, turn right at the traffic lights at Epping Road then left three kilometres later at the traffic lights at the *Pacific Highway*. Follow the Pacific Highway through the suburbs of Roseville, Lindfield, Killara and Gordon, then turn right at the signpost for St. Ives onto Mona Vale Road. Stay on Mona Vale Road through St. Ives, passing *Ku-ring-gai Wildflower Garden* on the left, (well

worth a visit in Spring), then some 10 kilometres later, shortly after passing the offices of Australian Geographic on the left, take the third turning on the left after the dual carriageway becomes a two-way traffic road, signposted for Church Point and West Head. The road soon enters bushland and becomes quite winding as it passes through stands of eucalyptus trees. Keep following the sign-posts for West Head, turning left over the wooden bridge over McCarr's Creek to the entrance to the National Park. Entry to the park is $4.00 per car. At the kiosk, at the entrance, the National Parks and Wildlife Officer on duty will be pleased to give you free pamphlets covering walks and tours, the location of aboriginal carvings and general information about *Ku-ring-gai Chase National Park*.

Stunning Views

Once past the kiosk, after a short distance turn right onto the road for *West Head* and follow it for 12 kilometres as it traverses a high sandstone bush covered plateau to *Commodore Heights* Look-Out on the tip of West Head. From this point you can enjoy the best scenic views to be found around Sydney, with the panoramas of Pittwater, the Warringah Peninsular and Palm Beach to the south and east and Broken Bay, Lion Island Nature Reserve, Brisbane Water National Park and Bouddi National Park to the north. Tame kookaburras that will eat from your hand make an amusing diversion at West Head if you tire of the views.

Returning by the same route to McCarr's Creek Road, follow it in an easterly direction as it skirts the picturesque suburb of *Church Point* on the shores of *Pittwater*. When Governor Phillip explored the area in March 1788, he noted that Pittwater was 'The finest piece of water I ever saw', and named it after the British Prime Minister Pitt the Younger.

Beaches Galore

Turn right at the traffic lights at Mona Vale to join the three lane highway of Pittwater Road; then after passing Mona Vale Golf course on the left,

turn left onto Coronation Street. Pass Mona Vale Hospital and keeping to the left, follow the road around the top of the headland past the small beaches of *Warriewood* and *Turimetta*, past a caravan and camping ground on the right, over the bridge at the entrance to *Narrabeen Lakes* and into Ocean Street. Pittwater Road follows the long five kilometre curve of *Narrabeen* and *Collaroy* Beaches. They are in fact one long beach, (the northern end is Narrabeen) and any of the 20 or so short roads you pass on the left running off Ocean Street and Pittwater Road, will take you to the beach and the pounding Pacific Ocean.

Collaroy Beach was named after the 'Collaroy', a coastal paddle-steamer that was blown onto the beach on January the 20th 1882. The ship stuck firmly in the sand and remained there for over two and a half years before it was refloated on September 19th 1884 and resumed its trading activities.

Narrabeen was the tram terminus on the Manly line between 1913 and 1939 when the line closed. D.H. Lawrence, who travelled on the tram from Manly in 1922, recounted in his novel 'Kangaroo', "The tram took them five or six miles to the terminus. This was the end of everywhere, with new 'stores' – that is fly-blown shops with corrugated iron roofs – and with a tram-shelter, and little house-agents' booths plastered with signs…". The tram shelter is still there at Narrabeen on Pittwater Road, now used as a bus shelter.

Passing through Collaroy shops then Long Reef Golf Links on the left, as Pittwater Road sweeps round to the right, *Dee Why Lagoon Wildfowl Reserve* can be seen below, while just to the left as you round the corner, is an access road to *Long Reef Beach*. On most days windsurfers can be seen practising wave-jumping just here. As Pittwater Road enters Dee Why, turn left into Dee Why Parade, follow it to the end to *Dee Why Beach*, then turn right to follow Griffen Road up and over the crest of a rise, from the top of which there is a view to Manly and North Head. After descending the hill and

crossing the bridge over *Harbord Lagoon*, drive straight on into Carrington parade, and follow it as it passes the southern end of *Curl Curl Beach*. Keep to the left to follow the road at the top of the cliff around McKillop Park, pass *Harbord Beach* below you on the left and join Evans Street.

Now it's just a question of setting your sights for Circular Quay. At the end of Evans Street turn left along Albert Street, through Harbord shops, then turn left at Oliver Street, turn left again at the bottom of Oliver Street at the traffic lights into Pittwater Road, at Manly Golf Links go straight on into Balgowlah Road and take the first right into Kenneth Road. At the first set of traffic lights on Kenneth Road turn left into Condamine Street and now you are virtually home and dry. This is the main highway to Sydney, just follow the signs for the next 12 kilometres to take you over the Spit and Harbour Bridges back to the City.

A walk on the Wild Side

Tonight if you still have the energy, grab a cab and go to *Kings Cross*. Kings Cross, or 'The Cross' as it is usually known in Sydney, was called Queen's Cross in 1897 after the Diamond Jubilee of Queen Victoria, then renamed Kings Cross in 1904 after Edward VII. The 'Cross' part of the title comes from the intersection of five roads at Kings Cross at the junction of William Street and Darlinghurst Road.

Kings Cross is certainly the King of vice in Sydney these days, with prostitutes hanging out on the street corners, a number of strip joints lining Darlinghurst Road and a flourishing drug trade on the streets. Although with that said, the Cross is the most lively area in Sydney for night life, boasting some good restaurants and nightclubs, with souvenir and other shops staying open until well into the night.

After a night on the town in Sydney it's nice to see the harbour at first light. Early morning activity on Sydney Harbour photographed from Potts Point near Kings Cross. The Canberra has just come through the heads, while off Bradley's Head a freighter is overtaken by the Manly Ferry on its way to Sydney. Another ferry and a hydrofoil go by in the opposite direction on their way to Manly as two tugs wait to pick up the Canberra when she passes by.

FRIDAY

Friday

In the steps of the First Fleeters

Today's itinerary includes a guided tour of the Opera House and a stroll through the historic Rocks area of Sydney.

From Circular Quay, follow Circular Quay East around the waterfront for a short distance, then cross the road to ascend *Moore Stairs* (1868) running up between two office blocks. Cross Macquarie Street to enter the park opposite, and taking the centre path go through the gates (open 8.00am to sunset) outside Government House, turn left and follow the road that skirts the grounds of Government House before entering the *Royal Botanic Gardens*. The grassy slope just here is a good location to take photos of the *Opera House*. Walk down the path, through the entrance gate to the Botanic Gardens and across the tarmac to the Opera House.

Sydney Opera House

The story of the Opera House is something of an Opera in itself. The English composer *Eugene Goosens*, a direct descendant of Captain Cook, was appointed Conductor of the Sydney Symphony Orchestra in 1947. Goosens persuaded the government of the day that Sydney should have its own Opera Theatre and that it should be built on Bennelong Point opposite the Harbour Bridge. In March 1956, the year following the announcement by the Government of Bennelong Point as the site for an Opera House, Goosens luggage was searched by Customs at the airport when he was returning from an overseas trip, and found to contain a quantity of pornographic photos, films and books. Goosens was tried and found guilty of importing indecent material, he resigned as conductor and left Australia that May.

Previous pages. Liner Queen Elizabeth II arrives at Circular Quay.

Following pages. The design of the Opera House looks as fresh today as when it was conceived by Jorn Utzon over 30 years ago between May-December 1956, "Whenever I could get time off from my other work."

Government House (below left) residence of the Governor of New South Wales, the Queen's representative in New South Wales. Members of the Royal Family often stay there while visiting Australia. The Tudor style structure with crenellations, tall chimneys and small towers was designed by London architect Edward Blore, special architect to William IV and then to Queen Victoria. The House was constructed 1837-45.

Tourists at the Opera House (left).

The shells of the Opera House (below) are coated with 1,056,000 tiles, in a mixture of matt and glossy finishes to cut down on glare. Utzon studied tiles from Asia and the Middle East before specifying a patented Swedish made self-cleaning tile for the Opera House that rinses clean with each rain shower.

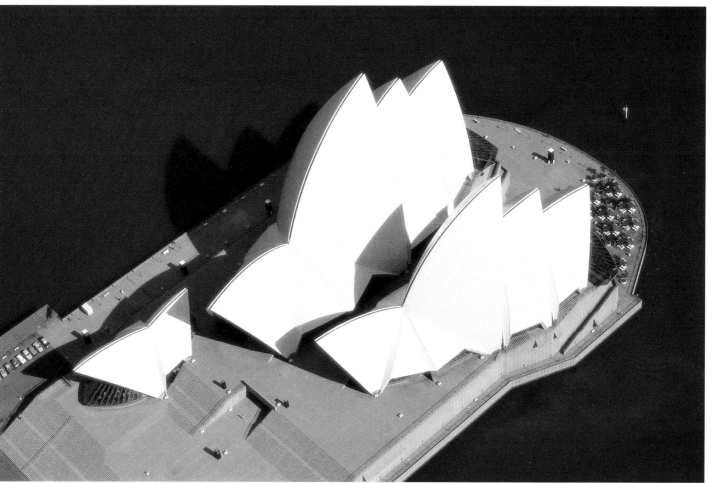

Previous pages. Sydney Opera House floodlit at dusk on Bennelong Point. Two days after the First Fleet landed, some cattle and horses were landed on a small island just off the eastern tip of Sydney Cove. A local aborigine, Ben Long, that Governor Phillip had captured to 'civilise' was housed on Cattle Island in a brick hut. In 1817 Macquarie built a fort on the island and linked it to the shore. In 1902 the fort was demolished to make way for a red-brick mock-gothic battlemented tram depot, which in turn came down in 1959 to make way for the Opera House. The land on which the Opera House stands has been known as Bennelong Point ever since Ben Long, the aborigine stayed there.

An international design competition for the Opera House, commissioned by the N.S.W. Government in 1957, with a first prize of £5,000, received 233 entries and was won by the unanimous choice of the four judges, by 38 year old Danish Architect *Jorn Utzon*. A team of quantity surveyors examined the top 10 designs from the competition, and worked out that Utzon's plan would cost about $7 million dollars to build, the cheapest they thought, of the 10 they looked at. It was decided that the Opera House would take 3 years to complete.

To finance the project, a public lottery 'The Opera House Lottery' was started. Tragedy struck when following the publicity surrounding the awarding of one of the first prizes of £100,000, the winner's son, eight year old Graeme Thorne, was kidnapped, held to ransom, then murdered after the ransom was paid.

Construction of the Opera House proceeded slowly, largely due to design and construction difficulties associated with the unique architecture of the project. In February 1966, with construction still proceeding on the Opera House shells, Utzon resigned following disagreements with the Minister of Public Works of a new Liberal State Government over the cost of the design of the interior of the Opera House and Concert Hall. Talking of 'malice in Blunderland' and later saying 'I do not care if they pull the Opera House

down', Utzon wrote in his letter of resignation '... there has been no collaboration on the most vital items of the job in the last many months from your department's side'.

Utzon's design for the interior of the Opera House was shelved, and the design of the interior and the completion of the project was overseen by a team of four Australian Architects.

By the time the Opera House was officially opened by the Queen on Saturday October 20, 1973, 15 years after construction started, the final cost of the project had increased to a cool $102 million. Jorn Utzon declined his invitation to attend the opening, and to date has never returned to Australia to see his completed masterpiece.

The 15 years following the completion of the Opera House have proved its success, not only as a design exercise, but as a performance venue. The acoustics of the Concert Hall are rated among the top three theatres in the world, while the complex of five theatres at the Opera House is one of the busiest performing arts centres in the world, with over 50,000 live performances already having been held there.

Opera House Tours

Guided tours of the Opera House leave approximately every 40 minutes, seven days a week, from the

The Opera House and Harbour Bridge from The Domain (above).

The glassed in foyers of the Opera House and Concert Hall (top left), offer panoramic views of the Harbour from inside (above left).

Circular Quay at night (following pages), a far cry from the scene that greeted Governor Phillip 200 years ago. Phillip chose Sydney Cove from the multitude of bays in the Harbour as the "one which had the finest spring of water, and in which ships can anchor ... close to the shore." He named it 'Sydney' after Thomas Townshend, First Viscount Sydney, British Home Secretary 1784-89.

George Street (top).

Cadman's Cottage (above) the oldest dwelling in Sydney, was built on the waterfront of Sydney Cove. However, land reclamations since then have pushed the sea 100 metres back.

lower concourse walkway on the south-west side of the Opera House. Prices are $5.50 adults, $3.00 concessions. Privately conducted tours are available for $75.00. Backstage tours, on Sundays only, cost $8.50. For further information call 250 7250.

Alternatively the Tourism and Marketing Department of the Opera House (phone 250 7111), organize a number of exciting outings. By booking tickets to performances through the department, visitors are presented with complimentary handmade Opera House chocolates on arrival and champagne at interval. Or, 'An Evening at the Sydney Opera House' ticket includes the performance, dinner and a guided

The Rocks Square on Playfair Street.

tour. Finally, you can buy a ticket for lunch at the Opera House with a mini-tour of the interior thrown in.

From the Opera House, return to Circular Quay, walk past the ferry wharves and turn right onto Circular Quay West to reach *Cadman's Cottage,* near the *Overseas Passenger Terminal.* An interesting alternative route to Cadman's Cottage would be to ascend Tarpeian steps in front of the Opera House Forecourt, walk through the park to Macquarie Street, ascend a flight of steps up to the *Cahill Expressway* footpath, and with an elevated view of *Circular Quay* follow the expressway to the stairs at Cumberland Street and wend your way through The Rocks to Cadman's Cottage.

First Fleeters and Convicts

The *Tarpeian Steps* received their name because the rock at the point

Friday

that they are cut from was jestingly referred to as the 'Tarpeian Rock' by the First Fleet Soldiers after the rock in Ancient Rome from which traitors were thrown to their death. The 'Tarpeian Way' next to the paling fence in the park at the top of the steps, was the route the convicts used after arriving in Sydney by ship to get to Hyde Park Barracks.

From the Cahill Expressway footpath there is a good view of the Circular Quay Area. On the left, the Overseas Passenger Terminal was the point where 100,000's of European migrants arriving in Australia disembarked in the 1950's and 1960's. In the 1950's when planning was going ahead for a new Passenger Terminal, the New South Wales minister for public works, J.J. Cahill, wanted to build it on the site of the tram depot at Bennelong Point, but Goosens persuaded Cahill that the Opera House should go at Bennelong Point and the Passenger Terminal should remain on the west side of the Cove.

South of the Passenger Terminal,

closer to the Expressway, was the first area of white settlement in Australia. When the 1,030 people of the First Fleet, including 500 male, 200 female convicts and 13 children, landed in January 1788, they cleared the bush, and built a bakery, a store, a hospital, men's and women's camps and huts for the soldiers from trees, bark and branches of local mimosa or 'wattle' as they called it after 'wattle and daub'.

The building of Circular Quay itself was supervised by Colonel George Barney, designer of Victoria Barracks. In a work that took 7 years, involved the labour of thousands of convicts and the quarrying of tens of thousands of tons of rock from Harbour Headlands, Islands and Argyle Cut, Barney reclaimed 5 hectares at the estuary of the Tank Stream, dredged Sydney Cove using the 'Hercules' a locally built steam dredge and built sea walls to form the horse-shoe shaped 'Semi-Circular Quay'.

The Rocks

Cadman's Cottage, unused and derelict in 1972, has been restored to resemble its original condition by the National Parks and Wildlife Service, who have an information centre inside. The cottage, the oldest dwelling in Sydney, was built in 1816 for John Cadman, transported to Australia in 1798 for stealing a horse. Cadman was made Government Coxswain by Macquarie, received a conditional pardon, and was later promoted to 'Superintendent of Government Boats', a post he held from 1827 to 1846, when he retired aged 88.

Walk up the steps next to Cadman's Cottage into George Street, turn right and after a short distance reach *The Rocks Visitors' Centre* at 104 George Street, inside the old Coroner's Court (1907). The Centre is a mine of information on The Rocks and has free maps and information booklets on the area. The Visitors' Centre is part of the Sydney Cove Redevelopment Authority, set up by an act of Parliament in 1968,

'To develop Sydney Cove as the Gateway to Sydney, keeping in mind the past, present and the future.'. Over the past 20 years the authority has completed a lot of useful work in The Rocks, restoring old buildings.

Continue on George Street and turn left into *Playfair Street*. The sandstone Union Bond Stores (1841), on the corner, containing a branch of the Westpac Bank with a banking museum upstairs, was designed by Ashley Alexander, designer of Dartmoor Prison in England.

Walk the length of Playfair Street and turn right into Argyle Street. *The Tourist Newsfront Office* on the left near the end of Playfair Street specialises in information on places to stay in Sydney and guided tours and holidays in and around Sydney. A short distance up Argyle Street you pass the entrance to the cobbled courtyard of the *Argyle Stores*. The cobblestones were brought out from England as ballast in the hulls of sailing ships.

One time owner of Argyle Stores, *Mary Reibey*, transported to Australia as a 13 year old girl, was the most influential business-woman and merchant in Sydney during the early part of last century. Among other things she worked in the setting up of the Bank of N.S.W. in 1815 (now Westpac Bank). A letter Mary Reibey wrote home to her Aunt on October 8, 1792, the day after she arrived on a convict transport in Sydney, is the earliest surviving letter written by an Australian convict.

The *Argyle Centre* in Argyle Stores has a number of craft, souvenir and bookshops on three levels of the old stores.

As you continue west on Argyle Street, walk through *Argyle Cut*. The Cut was started in 1843 by convict chain gangs, working by hand to cut rock for the seawalls and the infill at Circular Quay and was completed in 1859 by free labour using blasting. The stone Princes Street Bridge over the cut and the entire length of Princes Street with its houses was demolished when the Harbour Bridge approaches were built in the 1920s.

Emerge from Argyle Cut at *Argyle*

Argyle Stores in The Rocks (above far left), houses a bookshop, craftshops and souvenir shops.

The convict on the three sided 'First Impressions' sculpture (above left).

The Argyle Cut (above) was partly quarried by convicts.

Place, Sydney's only village green lined by a variety of styles of Georgian and Victorian cottages and terraces, erected between 1840 to 1880. Argyle Place was named in 1810 by Governor Macquarie after his home county in Scotland.

At the east end of Argyle Place near Argyle Cut, Holy Trinity Church known as the *'Garrison Church',* was used by soldiers of Dawes Point Battery. The first military church in Australia with a foundation stone laid in 1840, it was built from stone quarried by convicts at Argyle Cut. The Garrison Church was enlarged to a design by Edmund Blacket, completed 1878. A spire included in Blacket's design was never completed. The church is much roomier inside than it appears from the exterior and can seat 600. The east window of the church is considered the finest example of stained glass in Sydney.

Coming out of the church, cross Argyle Street, go up the steps next to the post box and follow Watson Road and Upper Fort Street to Observatory Hill.

The Observatory and Astronomer's Residence stand on the site of Fort Phillip Citadel, a hexagonal redoubt with sides 100 feet long started in 1804 by Governor King to be used as a last line of defence by the Government if there was an insurrection by political prisoners. However, the fort was never used and it didn't save Governor Bligh, who was overthrown by the military in 1808. The fort was demolished in the 1840s except for two of the walls which form part of the enclosure of the Sydney Observatory.

The telescopes in The Observatory were used for astronomical research from 1858 to 1982 when The Observatory closed. The building now houses a museum, and night viewings through the old telescopes can be booked by ringing 241 2478. A time ball on the weather vane on the tower of the Observatory dropped daily at 1pm as a signal for a cannon to be fired from Dawes Point and then Fort Denison between 1858 and 1942. The practice was stopped that year following the Japanese midget submarine attack on Sydney Har-

bour, as it was feared the noise might alarm Sydney residents.

In front of the Observatory near a bandstand, a memorial lists the names of men from the units of volunteers from N.S.W. who were killed in the Boer War. A rusting Krupp artillery piece in front of the memorial, captured during the war, was forged in Essen in 1895.

Walk south from the Observatory, skirting the cutting of the Cahill Expressway, to the *National Trust Centre;* since 1975 the headquarters of the N.S.W. Branch of the Australian National Trust. The Trust offices are located in a building built in 1815 as a Military Hospital by Governor Macquarie, designed by his young aide-de-camp, Lieutenant John Watts. Originally constructed with double-storeyed verandahs similar to the Mint Museum, the present neo-classical facade was added by colonial Architect Mortimer Lewis in 1871. When George Street Barracks moved to Victoria Barracks in 1848, the building was used for Fort Street Model School

Pier One (above), with a range of entertainments, shops and restaurants offers something for all-age groups.

Observatory Hill (above left). Note Argyle Green (lower centre), Argyle Church (left), the National Trust Centre and S. H. Ervin Gallery (top right) and Kent Street (right).

The Harbour Bridge from Observatory Hill (left).

The Garrison Church (far left) was attended by soldiers from nearby Dawes Point Battery.

The Lord Nelson was built as a residence in 1834, then converted into a hotel in 1842.

from 1849 to 1974. Behind the main building, the S.H. Ervin Gallery of Australian Art and Architecture is housed in an old ward added to the military hospital in 1841.

Australia's Oldest Pub

Backtracking the same way you come towards the Observatory, descend *Agar Steps* to Kent Street next to the road cutting carrying the traffic from the Cahill Expressway up to the Harbour Bridge, turn right and walk to Argyle Place, then fork left off Argyle Place into Lower Fort Street. Pass the *Hero of Waterloo Hotel* on the corner of Windmill Street, the oldest pub in Australia (1809) and the Colonial House museum at 53 Lower Fort Street (open 10am to 5pm daily), walk right to the end of Lower Fort Street and over the bridge crossing Hickson Road into Pier One.

Pier One on the harbour within spitting distance of the Harbour Bridge, occupies the old Walsh Bay Wharf No. 1, completed in 1912, 20 years before the opening of the Harbour Bridge. Converted into Pier One in 1982, the old wharf now houses souvenir and jewellery shops, an amusement arcade and eateries catering for all budgets, from cheap Chinese food to two first rate restaurants that enjoy unsurpassed harbour views.

Exit Pier One on the ground floor and follow Hickson Road round to *Dawes Point Park,* dominated by the south pylons of the Harbour Bridge and the tall piers supporting the elevated Bradfield Highway. Lieutenant William Dawes of the first fleet constructed a gun battery on the point in 1788 using six naval cannons from the Sirius. Dawes, a scientist, had been sent to the colony by the Astronomer Royal to observe Maskelyn's Comet, due to appear in the southern skies late in 1788.

The Waterfront Restaurant in Campbell's Storehouse, on the harbour at Circular Quay opposite the Opera House.

A telescope Dawes set up for astronomical observations came to more practical use when it was used to watch signals from the flag station near South Head.

Dawes Battery was enlarged to include five mortars, thirteen 42 pounders, a magazine, soldiers' quarters and a residence for the C.O. These structures were demolished when the bridge was built, and all that remains today are five cannons cast in 1843 and 1844 resting peacefully on carriages on the grassy slope of the park overlooking the harbour and Opera House.

Continue on Hickson Road, forking left onto Circular Quay West to *Campbell's Storehouse.* Robert Campbell built the first private wharf in the colony here and ran a prosperous merchant's business from his stores on the waterfront. Campbell's wharf was better built than those provided by the colony's administrators. An officer from HMS Glatton, who had to strengthen the Government Hospital wharf to unload some guns in 1806, declared 'The only good landing place that has respectable appearance has been erected by a Mr. Robert Campbell.' Two restaurants and a wine bar have been tastefully incorporated to blend in with the fabric of the old stores.

That's the end of today's tour. If you have covered even half the ground no doubt you will be worn out and thoroughly deserve a pep-up in the evening by making your way to the Inter-Continental Hotel on the corner of Macquarie and Bridge Street. From the Cocktail Lounge in the Top of the Treasury Bar on the 31st level, open every night, you can enjoy spectacular views of the Botanical Gardens, Circular Quay, the Opera House and Government House to the accompaniment of a local jazz band.

Friday

SATURDAY

Darling Harbour and the City's best view

Start the day at Sydney's Chinatown; see if you can resist the enticing
aromas wafting through the doors of the many restaurants.
After seeing the Chinese Gardens, Festival Markets and museums at
Darling Harbour, catch a ride on the monorail to the ritzy shopping centre
of Sydney, taking in the Queen Victoria Building and Centrepoint on the way.
Then cross Hyde Park and the Domain to the Art Gallery of N.S.W.,
and finish the afternoon with a visit to Fort Denison on Sydney Harbour,
or with a Captain Cook Cruise on the Harbour.

Hail a cab to *Dixon Street* in the centre of Sydney's *Chinatown*. Many of the restaurants offer a Chinese breakfast if you've missed your breakfast. Nearby, on the corner of Hay Street and Harbour Street, the *Sydney Entertainment Centre*, the largest indoor auditorium in Australia, opened in 1983 and seating up to 12,500 is a venue for concerts, ice skating events, indoor tennis tournaments and so on. To find out who's in town and to make bookings go to the booking office in the Entertainment Centre or ring Mitchells Bass on 266 4800.

Turn left after the Entertainment Centre. On your right is the historic Pump House which formerly provided hydraulic pressure to operate lifts in the city. The building now accomodates the refurbished Tavern and Boutique Brewery. Here you can see beer being brewed 'on sight', though it's probably a little too early to taste the first drop!

The Powerhouse Museum

Continue along Little Pier Street, up a ramp and follow the arrows to the Powerhouse Museum. A science and transport museum, the Powerhouse has over 11,000 objects on display, including the heaviest item, a ten ton steam locomotive that ran on Sydney's first rail line between Sydney and Parramatta; the tallest, a 10 metre high Boulton and Watt steam engine; and the widest, a Catalina flying boat with a wingspan of 32 metres. The Powerhouse is open 10.00 am to 5.00 pm daily, (closed Christmas Day and Good Friday).

The Chinese Gardens

Make your way back towards the Pump House and walk under Pier Street to the southern end of Darling Harbour. Continue walking and after a short distance you can see on your right the Chinese Gardens. The "Garden of Friendship" was designed according to southern Chinese tradition by Sydney's sister city, Guangzhou in China. A double-storey pavilion, "the Gurr", stands above a surrounding system of interconnected lakes and waterfalls. Follow the pathways around the landscaped gardens and over bridges before resting at the Tea House where the scent of lotus flowers mingles with that of freshly brewed tea and traditional cakes. The Garden is open Monday to Friday 10.00 am to sunset and weekends 9.30 am to sunset.

The Exhibition Centre

Leaving the Gardens, walk through Tumbalong Park with its fountains and groves of native eucalypts. The Port Jackson Fig tree within the park is affectionately known as "Fred". On the left of the park lies the Exhibition Centre which covers a massive 25,000 square metres of column-free space under the one roof. Opened in January 1988, the Centre is designed to hold major international exhibitions. The glassed eastern facade is stepped back in five separate stages that can be partitioned off to form smaller halls. The fifth hall is linked by covered walkway to the Convention Centre. Continue north along walkways lined by palm trees and pass under the flyover to Cockle Bay.

On the left the seven storey Convention Centre provides seating for 3,500 people and houses modern communications, translation and audio/visual equipment that gives it the technology demanded on the international convention circuit. Inside the Centre a restaurant and bar overlook the Waterfront Promenade and Cockle Bay.

Harbourside Festival Markets

Continue your stroll alongside Cockle Bay. On your left the Har-

Centrepoint Tower (right).

Previous pages. Sydney City from the south with Hyde Park and St Mary's Cathedral on the right.

97

Sydney Convention Centre (right).

New Year's Eve fireworks at Cockle Bay, Darling Harbour (far right).

The 'Garden of Friendship' Chinese Gardens (bottom).

The TNT monorail (below), runs in a 3.6 kilometre loop through city streets and around Darling Harbour.

99

101

bourside Festival Market Place has 200 shops to tease your wallet and 54 assorted food outlets to tempt your palate. The Market is open from Monday to Saturday 10.00 am to 9.00 pm and Sunday 10.00 am to 6.00 pm. Restaurants trade until 2.00 am.

The National Maritime Museum

Walk underneath Pyrmont Bridge to the new National Maritime Museum, which focuses on the history of Australia's links with the sea from earliest times to the present. Alongside the museum's two wharves you can see a number of ships including the 'Vampire', a former RAN destroyer and 'Akarana', a restored 1888 11.9

metre gaff cutter which was New Zealand's Bicentennial gift to Australia.

Sydney Aquarium

From Harbourside catch a boat ride across Cockle Bay to the Sydney Aquarium where 50 tanks and two walk-through oceanariums house 350 species from Harbour prawns to saltwater crocodiles and the infamous Aussie shark. Open daily from 9.30 am to 9.00 pm.

The Monorail

Take the escalator up to Pyrmont Bridge, designed by Australian engineers at the turn of the century, walk back to Harbourside and catch

the Monorail for an aerial view of Darling Harbour. Built by TNT Harbourlink in 1988, the Monorail runs in a 3.6 kilometre loop and has six stations: Harbourside, Convention, Haymarket, World Square, Park Plaza (Town Hall) and City Centre. Buy a $2.00 token at the station entrance for a round trip. Children under 4 years old travel free. The service runs 8.00 am to 9.00 pm Sunday to Thursday and 8.00 am to 11.00 pm Friday and Saturday.

St. Andrew's Cathedral

Alight at Park Plaza (Town Hall). Outside the station, turn right into Pitt Street then right again at Park Street and at George Street turn left and walk to *St. Andrews Cathedral*. The

foundation stone of the cathedral was laid by Governor Macquarie on August 31, 1819, but construction was axed on the recommendation of Colonial Commissioner Bigge and the project wasn't restarted until 1837. Architect Edmund Blacket redesigned the Cathedral in "perpendicular gothic" style based on St. Mary's Church in Oxford England. The Cathedral was consecrated on St. Andrew's Day, November 30, 1868.

Edmund Thomas Blacket, (1817 to 1883), designer of the University, St. Andrew's and many other churches in Sydney, was buried originally in Balmain Cemetery. When the Cemetery was turned into a park in 1941, the ashes of Blacket and his

The Exhibition Centre (top left) covers 25,000 square metres of column-free space under one roof. Tumbalong Park is in the foreground.

Sydney Aquarium (bottom left) houses 350 species from Harbour prawns to Aussie sharks.

The TNT Harbourlink Monorail on Pyrmont Bridge (above).

Downtown Sydney (above).

Sydney Entertainment Centre (above right), Australia's largest indoor auditorium.

Centrepoint Tower from Kingsford Smith Airport (left).

wife were re-interred under the floor in the south west corner of the Cathedral. On the north wall inside the Cathedral hangs a Union Jack which was carried by Mr. R. Fair of the Australian 8th Division while a P.O.W. in Singapore, on the Burma Railway, and to the coal mines of Ohama in Japan, where it was flown on V.J. Day 1945 after taking down the Japanese flag.

Continuing north on George Street, walk past the Italian Renaissance styled Sydney Town Hall, opened in 1889. Before the Opera House was completed the Town Hall's Centennial Hall, with seating for 2,000, was Sydney's main concert venue. Famous organists go into raptures over the tonal excellence of the Centennial Hall's organ, one of the two largest original 19th century organs in the world, with 8,500 pipes.

The Queen Victoria Building

Cross Druitt Street to the *Queen Victoria* Building, a real cathedral of a shopping centre built in the 19th century, occupying an entire city block between York and George Streets and containing 200 shops and restaurants. Sydney's, and some of the world's leading ladies' and mens' fashion houses are all collected together under one roof. Sit at one of the tables of the Old Vienna Coffee House on the landing at the north end of the Albert Walk, listen to the classical piped music and wallow in the atmosphere of Victorian splendour.

Continue north on George Street, turn right at Market Street and enter the foyer of the State Theatre at 49 Market Street; a typical lavishly decorated pre-war picture palace, opened in 1929. The foyer of the theatre has brass doors with filigree panels, the staircase and columns are solid marble and beneath the central dome St. George and the Dragon are locked in combat on the mosaic floor. Built to seat 3,000, the theatre is used these days for live performances and conventions, while the foyer is in demand as a set for movies and commercials and for holding dinner and cocktail parties.

Sydney Tower

Cross Market Street and walk across the Pitt Street Mall to *Centrepoint*. Go up three flights of escalators to the Podium Level, where lifts leave for the Sydney Tower Observation Deck ($5.00 adults, $3.00 children), or one floor down the Gallery Level, is the access point for lifts to the revolving restaurants (no lift charge).

Centrepoint is much more than just an observation tower. The ground floor and lower levels comprise a shopping centre with over 170 speciality shops, including many eateries on the Pitt Street level. This centre is linked by overhead walkways and underground promenades to the David Jones and Grace Bros Department Stores, flanking Centrepoint to the east and west. A 10 storey office building and a convention and exhibition centre sit on top of the Centrepoint retail levels.

The tower itself, rising 1,000 feet (304.8 metres) above street level, is slightly higher than the Eiffel Tower and the tallest building south of the equator. Its golden turret has a wai-

Dixon Street (above) in the centre of Sydney's Chinatown in The Haymarket, a suburb in the south of the City where Sydney's Chinese community congregated after leaving The Rocks late last century.

George Street (right), the High Street of Governor Phillip's day.

ter service revolving restaurant, a cheaper informal self-select revolving restaurant, a function room and an observation level.

An exciting building in its design, many innovative techniques were employed in the construction of Sydney Tower. The stem is made from 46 barrel-shaped steel units stacked one on top of the other. The crowning golden turret and its white telecommunications antenna together weighing nearly 2,000 tonnes, are locked onto the top of the stem, and anchored to the concrete roof of

Centrepoint by 56 long steel cables, made in Australia under a Swiss patent.

A 162,000 litre water tank, suspended on cables in the turret linked to mechanical dampers, oscillates at the same frequency as the tower but out of phase with it to minimise the sway of the tower in strong winds. It is amazing how effective this system is, for the tower stays as stiff as a ram-rod even in the most blustery conditions.

Descending from the tower, from

St Andrews Cathedral (above), with a foundation stone laid by Governor Macquarie on 31st August 1819, is the oldest cathedral in Australia. However, construction was abandoned on the recommendation of Colonial Commissioner Bigge, and the present structure was built between 1837-68.

The interior of the Queen Victoria Building (below). Animated scenes featuring events from the British Royal Family's past light up inside the clock on the hour, and are visible from the top gallery.

The Queen Victoria Building (far right) designed by Sydney City Council Architect George McRae in Romanesque style to resemble a Byzantine Palace as a 'municipal market on the scale of a cathedral', was constructed between 1893 and 1898. The market was not a commercial success, and in the 1930s the interior galleries were concreted over and partitioned for council offices, and the Sydney City Library. After talk of pulling the 'monstrosity' down, it was decided the Queen Victoria Building should be preserved. The Malaysian company Ipoh Garden Berhad carried out a mammoth restoration project between January 1984 and November 1986 at a cost of 80 million dollars, in return for a 99 year lease on the site.

109

Centrepoint Tower from Hyde Park (right).

The City at dusk, (far right) from the Eastern Suburbs.

the Gallery Level of Centrepoint (green carpet) walk through the shops and over the enclosed pedestrian bridge spanning Castlereagh Street into *David Jones*. Go down the escalator to the ground floor, and be prepared to mislay your credit cards, because the entire ground floor, in a most elegant grey marble setting, is devoted to the sale of everything for the well-dressed lady, with belts, stockings, handbags, jewellery, perfumes and cosmetics in abundance.

Fountains and Churches

Cross Elizabeth Street into *Hyde Park*. Set aside by Governor Phillip as a common 'never to be granted or let lease on', and called Hyde Park by Governor Macquarie after Hyde Park in London. Macquarie's Highlanders cleared the bush and laid out Sydney's first racecourse, 2 kilometres long. The park was also the site of Sydney's first cricket pitch. Walk past the *Archibald Fountain,* a collection of Greek Gods spouting water and cross College Street to *St. Mary's Cathedral.*

The site of St. Mary's was granted by Governor Macquarie to the first official chaplain to the colony of N.S.W., Father Joseph Therry who arrived in 1820. Macquarie laid the foundation stone of the Cathedral the following year. The original St. Mary's burnt down on June 29 1865 and all that remains is part of a pillar east of the present church near the entrance to the crypt. New designs were drawn up by architect William Wardell, construction was started in 1868, the Cathedral was in use by 1882 and was finished September 2, 1928. Two spires topping the south facing towers that were part of the design, were never completed.

Visitors are welcome to walk around the Cathedral except when services are on. Guided tours of the Cathedral take place the first Sunday of every month, or a self-guide booklet about the Cathedral can be picked up inside. The inlay of the floor of the crypt (open office hours only) and the mosaic floor of the sanctuary are worth seeing. The stained glass windows were made by Hardman Bros in England. The bells of St. Mary's, cast in the foundry of Whitechapel London in 1985 and installed June 1986, are the sister peal to Canterbury Cathedral in England.

The Art Gallery

From St. Mary's walk north on College Street into Prince Albert Road past the Tudor style Registrar General Department building, enter the Domain at Art Gallery Road and walk past the statue of Burns to the *Art Gallery of New South Wales.* Open Monday to Saturday from 10.00 am to 5.00 pm, Sundays from 12.00 pm to 5.00 pm and Wednesdays from 10.00 am to 8.00 pm for special exhibitions. Entry to the Art Gallery is free, although if a travelling world exhibition is on display there may be a charge for that section. The Gallery has permanent exhibitions on 18th to 20th century Australian Art, British Watercolours, 17th to 20th century European Art, Neo-Classical Sculptures and Asian Art.

A new wing in the Gallery opened

The Archibald Fountain (top), erected in 1932, was bequeathed to the people of Australia by J. F. Archibald, publisher of The Bulletin magazine to commemorate the association of Australia and France in the 1914-18 war. The figures from Greek Mythology are by Paris Sculptor François Sicard.

The Art Gallery of New South Wales (above).

A football game at lunchtime on a weekday in The Domain (top right).

The statue of Burns in the Domain, and St Mary's Cathedral (above right).

in December 1988. Its four levels include a sculpture garden, contemporary collections of Australian and European prints and drawings, 20th century British and European art, an impressionist exhibition as well as a new coffee shop and theatre space.

Fort Denison

If there's still time, you may wish to round off the day with a visit to *Fort Denison* conducted by the Maritime Services Board. Tours leave from Circular Quay at 10.15am, 12.15am and 2.00pm Tuesday to Sunday, although you will certainly need to book in advance by ringing Captain Cook Cruises on 251 5007. Alternatively, if you've had enough of colonial relics, a *Captain Cook Cruise* can

be booked on the same number.

When the First Fleet arrived in Sydney, 'Rock Island', as it was then known, was a convenient place to punish recalcitrant convicts, who were left in chains on the island for a week on bread and water. In November 1796 an Irish convict, Francis Morgan, who had been found guilty of a particularly brutal murder, was rowed out to the island and hanged and his body left to rot on the gallows as a deterrent to others. Before he was despatched, folklore has it that upon being asked if he had anything further to say, Morgan calmly surveyed the scenery from the top of Rock Island and said, 'Well it certainly is a fine harbour you have here.'.

One night in December 1839 two American warships that sailed into the harbour were only noticed when their presence was revealed at first light the following morning. To improve harbour defences, Governor Gipps ordered that a fort be built on Rock Island. The island was quarried to the waterline but the necessary funds were not forthcoming from the British Government and it wasn't until 1855, and the onset of the Crimean War, that construction of the fort finally went ahead. Colonel George Barney, who built Victoria Barracks and Circular Quay, designed the fort. The martello tower was designed by Government Architect Edmund Blacket. When it was opened in 1857 the fort was named after the Governor of N.S.W., Sir William Denison.

The guns of the fort were never fired in anger, although the fort once came under fire, albeit accidentally. During the Japanese midget submarine attack on Sydney in 1942, a shell from the American cruiser U.S.S. Chicago, fired at one of the submarines, hit Fort Denison's martello tower leaving a crack that can still be seen in the top of the tower wall.

Tonight, return to George Street and descend the stairs between the escalators at the entrance to the Hilton Hotel opposite the central dome of the Queen Victoria Building, to the Marble Bar in the base-

U.S. Sailors and local girls outside the Art Gallery during the 75th Anniversary celebrations of the Royal Australian Navy in October 1986.

ment. (Open Monday 12.00 pm to 1.00 pm, Tuesday and Wednesday 12.00 pm to 12.00 am, Thursday 12.00 pm to 1.00 am, Friday 12.00 pm to 2.00 am, Saturday 7.00 pm to 2.00 am and closed Sunday.

The bar was originally part of the 1890 Adams Hotel, owned by George Adams, a farm labourer from Hertfordshire who made a fortune holding public sweepstakes on horse races in the 1880's. Determined to

The guided tour of Fort Denison (top).

Fort Denison (below). The magazine where explosives were stored and the gun room with its three canons in the martello tower, look just the same today as when the Fort was completed in 1858. The Fort is the central tide register for New South Wales and the caretaker is responsible for taking readings from the measuring equipment in a room next to the martello tower. During the Second World War two anti-aircraft guns were mounted on the Fort, one on top of the martello tower and one on the west battlement, (bottom left of picture).

make the bar of his hotel the most opulent in Sydney and with money no object, Adams spent the then astronomical sum of £32,000 decorating his bar in 15th century Italian renaissance style. Fireplaces and columns were solid marble and the walls were hung with a series of 18 paintings by the Australian artist Julian Ashton featuring countryside scenes replete with voluptuous nudes. The twin bars of American walnut were sculptured with figures that amply complemented the paintings.

When the George Adams Hotel was demolished in 1968 the bar was classified by the National Trust as a First- Class Monument. The bar and all the marble fittings of the interior were painstakingly dismantled and numbered then re-erected in the basement of the Hilton Hotel ready for its opening in 1973.

The fact that fourteen of the original eighteen Julian Ashton nudes still decorate the Marble Bar's walls, perchance contributed to the bar winning Australian Playboy's survey for Best Bar in Australia in 1986.

Captain Cook Cruises 'City of Sydney'.

Saturday

SUNDAY

Exclusive suburbs and magnificent beaches

Leaving Circular Quay then walking through the Royal Botanic Gardens, today's route includes a stop at Elizabeth Bay House, a journey by cab around the exclusive harbourside eastern suburbs of Darling Point and Point Piper, a trip by flying boat from Rose Bay to Palm Beach, then a return journey back to Sydney through the northern beaches, and via the scenic Wakehurst Parkway and Eastern Valley Way.

Walk south on Phillip Street at the eastern end of Circular Quay, then turn left up Albert Street. Pass the *Police and Courts Museum* on the corner, occupying the old sandstone Water Police Station and Courthouse, which was used from 1854 to 1984. Turn right on Macquarie Street and pass the east facade of the Treasury, which is now part of the Intercontinental Hotel. Although quite small in proportion, the sandstone treasury with its marble columned portico has a demeanour befitting its original status. Turn left, and following the road to the rear of the N.S.W. Conservatorium of Music, enter through the gate into the Royal Botanic Gardens.

The site of the gardens was the first place in Sydney to be successfully cultivated by members of the First Fleet. By July 1788 on some alluvial soil either side of a small stream that ran into Farm Cove, a Government Farm had been established with 'nine acres of corn'. One of the Tolpuddle Martyrs, Joseph Gerrald, transported in 1794, built a cottage and farmed the area. Gerrald died in 1796 and was buried east of the creek.

Mrs Macquarie's Road

In 1816 Governor Macquarie completed a road about three kilometres long that ran from Old Government House around Farm Cove to the Point and back to Government House. Macquarie's wife, *Jane Austen*, made daily journeys in her carriage on the road and would stop at the point to relax and admire the scenery. That same year Macquarie appointed Charles Fraser, a soldier from his 46th Regiment of Highlanders to the post of 'Superintendent of the Botanic Gardens'.

Fraser visited Norfolk Island and New Zealand, Tasmania, West Australia and Queensland collecting plants and seeds and exchanged seeds with other botanists overseas. Fraser died in 1831. His successor, Richard Cunningham was speared to death by aborigines on the Bogan River collecting plant specimens whilst on Thomas Mitchell's expedition of 1835. Ever since, an appointment as live in Superintendent of the Botanic Gardens has been accepted with pride and as an honour, with most Superintendents holding the post for 20 or more years. Charles Moore enjoyed a particularly long stint as Superintendent for 48 years from 1848-1896.

The Gardens were renamed the Royal Botanic Gardens following the visit of *Queen Elizabeth* in 1954, the first reigning British Monarch to visit the country. She stepped ashore in Sydney at the Botanic Gardens on the east side of Farm Cove.

Amble through the gardens at will, to arrive at Mrs. Macquarie's Point. Which ever direction you take the Gardens are delightful. The

Barrenjoey Lighthouse at Palm Beach (previous pages).

Sulphur crested cockatoos (right) that frequent the Botanic Gardens, are quite a menace, uprooting plants and causing expensive damage to nearby roof-tops.

The Royal Botanic Gardens on Farm Cove (below), are one of the longest established botanical gardens in the western world, dating from 1816.

119

Australian native plants have the blue labels. Lookout for some of the 95 species of birds that have been seen in the Gardens over the years, you have a good chance of spotting the common ones, Kookaburras, Sulphur crested Cockatoos, white ibis, Indian Myna and the blue wren. At dusk brush-tailed possums come out and at certain times of the year flying fox bats descend on the Gardens in great numbers.

Next to the creek just south of the kiosk, in the centre of the gardens, a small plaque marks the site of the first Government Farm. On the east side of Farm Cove near the Fleet Stairs, a plain sandstone wall decorated with the Royal Crest commemorates the landing of Queen Elizabeth in 1954.

At the bus stop on Mrs. Macquarie's Road near the Point, the regular *Sydney Explorer Bus* can be picked up which will take you to Elizabeth Bay House. Alternatively, it's about half an hour's walk. If you opt for the latter, follow the path around the Point, past *Mrs. Macquarie's Chair,* a seat cut in the rock where Elizabeth Henriette Campbell used to wile away many hours enjoying the scenery. Some rock alcoves in the sandstone next to the path were used as shelters by unemployed, homeless men during the depression. After five minutes walk you will pass The Andrew (Boy) Charlton Pool on Woolloomooloo Bay. In 1924, 16-year-old Andrew Charlton beat Arne Borg the Swedish World Champion in a race at the Domain Baths, just here. Charlton went on to win a gold and silver medal at the Paris Olympics.

Azaleas in bloom in the gardens in spring (far left).

Elizabeth Campbell, wife of Governor Macquarie, used to ride from Government House in her carriage to the stone bench (above), to sit and gaze at the harbour.

The City from The Domain (left).

A few minutes walk after passing the pool, descend a flight of concrete steps past an electric sub-station into Lincoln Crescent, turn left along Cowper Wharf Roadway passing the Bells Hotel and Woolloomooloo Bay Hotel, then as you turn into Brougham Street ascend the broad flight of *McElhone Stairs* directly in front.

Garden Island

Walking through the gardens on Woolloomooloo Bay and as you climb McElhone Stairs you will no doubt have noticed some destroyers and other ships moored at *Garden Island Naval Base*. As its name implies, the base was once an 11 acre island lying 200 metres off Potts Point.

When the First Fleet landed the sailors from HMS Sirius cleared the vegetation on part of the island for a vegetable garden, hence the name. On some rocks on top of the island the initials of some of the sailors have been carved with the date 1788. The calling cards of these First Fleet Kilroys are protected by three glass pyramids.

The liner 'Canberra' berthed at Woolloomooloo Bay (above).

Ships at Garden Island naval base (right) during the 75th Anniversary of the Royal Australian Navy in October 1986. The battleship in the foreground is the U.S.S. Missouri. In 1945 the Japanese surrender was signed on the deck of the Missouri in Tokyo Bay.

In 1857 the island was granted by the NSW Government to the Royal Navy for use as a base. A number of buildings dating from around this time including residences, a barracks, a factory, stores and administration buildings still exist. In 1904 Garden Island was handed over to the Australian Commonwealth. It has been Australia's biggest naval base ever since, playing an important role as a re-supply depot for allied shipping through two World Wars.

On May 31, 1942, three Japanese midget submarines entered Sydney Harbour. A torpedo fired at ships moored at Garden Island, hit the wharf next to the Kuttabul, an old ferry being used as a dormitory,

blowing off the stern of the ferry and killing 19 ratings. Two of the submarines were sunk by depth charges, the third was never found. The two damaged submarines were recovered and their best halves were welded together to make a complete submarine, which takes pride of place outside the Australian War Memorial in Canberra.

Between 1940 and 1944 the island was joined to the mainland by the reclamation of 14 hectares of seabed during the building of the *Captain Cook Dry Dock,* a considerable feat of engineering at the time. Garden Island tours take place on the first Sunday of every month, 'phone 359 2371 for bookings.

Elizabeth Bay House (above), built between 1835-38 for Colonial Secretary Alexander Macleay, was considered the finest house in the colony. Designed as a 'Grecian Villa' with a surrounding verandah, the house was never completed to architect John Verge's drawings because the cost of the house bankrupted Macleay.

Elizabeth Bay House

At the top of McElhone Stairs cross leafy Victoria Street walk to the end of Challis Avenue, cross Macleay Street, walk through the alley opposite and turn right on Onslow Avenue to reach *Elizabeth Bay House.*

Elizabeth Bay House, in a quiet cul-de-sac on Elizabeth Bay, with a view overlooking the harbour, is a world away from the sleaze of Kings Cross just around the corner. The unpretentious exterior gives no clue to the treasure-trove of antiques within. The domed saloon of Elizabeth Bay House and elliptical stairway are considered particularly excellent examples of colonial architecture.

In October 1826, *Alexander John Macleay*, who had recently arrived from England to take up a post as Colonial Secretary was granted 54 acres of land at Elizabeth Bay. Macleay employed the architect John Verge to design a 'Grecian Villa' for the site. Built between 1835 and 1838 the completed house was regarded as the finest in the colony.

When the house passed out of the ownership of the Macleay Family early this century, the rot quickly set in. A Botanical Garden surrounding the house was engulfed by development, the kitchen wing was demolished and the house was successively a colony for artists, a venue for society weddings and dances, partitioned and turned into 15 flats and

finally an unused residence for the Lord Mayor of Sydney. The rot stopped in 1977, when the Historic Houses Trust of NSW acquired Elizabeth Bay House and painstakingly restored it to the period 1838-1845.

In 1845 when Alexander Macleay was in financial trouble, he sold the house to his son and the contents were sold to furnish the newly completed Government House. An inventory made of the contents at the time still exists, so it has been possible faithfully to reproduce the furnishings of the period. In 1873 William John Macleay, Alexander Macleay's son's cousin, donated the family's insect, botanical, anthropological and geological collections to Sydney University where they can be viewed today in the Macleay Museum.

Rushcutter's Bay

Hail a cab and head east on Bayswater and New South Head Road. After descending the hill from Kings Cross, pass on the left a wide expanse of park fronting onto *Rushcutters Bay*, where hundreds of yachts are berthed at several marinas.

Rushcutters Bay Park is on reclaimed marshland that once extended inland from the Bay. In May 1788 two convicts who were sent to cut rushes for thatch at the Bay, were killed by aborigines and had their tools stolen.

The view of Sydney Harbour (above) from the verandah of Elizabeth Bay House. The regular 'Sydney Explorer' bus service, operating on a route around the main tourist attractions in the city, is in the foreground.

125

St Mark's Church, Darling Point (right)

Terraced houses on Roslyn Gardens (below) near Elizabeth Bay House.

Rushcutter's Bay (previous pages).

Darling Point

Turn left on Darling Point Road. Pass *St. Mark's Church* on the right, where Elton John was married and the *'Swifts'* on the left, a crenellated mansion similar to Government House built last century for the owner of a brewery and until recently the official residence of the Catholic Archbishop of Sydney. At the end of Darling Point Road, the recently opened *McKell Park* enjoys good views of the Harbour and nearby Clark Island.

Backtrack on Darling Point Road and turn left at St. Mark's Church into Greenoaks Avenue, Pass *'Bishops-Court'* on the right, residence of the Anglican Archbishop of Sydney, turn left at Ocean Avenue, right at William Street past *Double Bay* and then left at the end of William Street to rejoin New South Head Road. After a short distance turn left on Wolseley Road and make a quick circuit of *Point Piper* on Wyuna and Wunulla Roads; who knows where they get the names from, but these unlikely addresses include some of the most valuable harbourside homes in Sydney.

Rose Bay

Rejoining New South Head Road pay off the cab at *Lyne Park* on *Rose Bay*. The tiny Police Station at Rose Bay Park on the corner of Wunulla Road and New South Head Road was once the lodge for Woollahra House (1871), pulled down by developers before the war.

Rose Bay has been associated with flying contraptions since the very earliest days of man made flight. *Lawrence Hargrave* the pioneer plane designer whose portrait appears on the back of the Australian $20.00 note, had a house at Point Piper overlooking Rose Bay and would fly kites over the Bay testing his designs. Later, Rose Bay became Sydney's International Airport. Before the War 'Empire' flying boats of Imperial Airways and Qantas Airways offered services to the U.K. and across the Tasman to New Zealand.

It is thought that the flying boat base was the target of a Japanese submarine that surfaced off Bondi Beach and shelled Rose Bay on the night of June 7, 1942. Regular flying boat services continued to operate from Rose Bay to Norfolk and Lord Howe Islands until 1974.

A trip by flying boat

Why, you are no doubt asking yourself, are we coming out to Rose Bay when, if you've been faithfully following this guide, we already passed this way on Tuesday returning to Sydney from Vaucluse House. The answer is, to take a flight on one of *Aquatic Airways'* flying boats from Rose Bay to Palm Beach.

Aquatic Airways seven seater DeHavilland Beavers and ten seater Amphibious Nomads, fly four times each way Monday to Friday from Rose Bay to Palm Beach and twice each way on Saturdays and Sundays. Flights to the Hawkesbury district, to Gosford and pleasure flights are also available.

The tiny DeHavilland Beavers, a plane produced from the late 1940s to 1967, look as if they've been transported from another time and place. Indeed in a way they have. One was purchased by Aquatic Airways from the United States and the other was bought from the Ghana Air Force where it had been used as a spotter plane.

The cost of flights is $40.00 each way; call Aquatic Airways on 919 5966 or 371 7700 to make bookings.

First Class Restaurants

If you want to do things in real style, charter an Aquatic Airways flight to take you to one of the restaurants on the Hawkesbury Estuary in the vicinity of Palm Beach. The restaurants front onto the water and the plane will taxi to the pontoon at the restaurant so you can alight directly at your destination. There are several choices including Flamingoes, McClues Riverside Restaurant, Peat's Bite and what's generally regarded as one of the best restaurants in Australia,

The Berowra Waters Inn. Alternatively there is Jonahs, overlooking Whale Beach, a short free ride in a taxi by road from Palm Beach.

Separate arrangements must be made for the restaurant and the flight. Prices for the restaurants reflect the standard of food and service and with all the trimmings and wine, expect to pay $60 to $100 per head.

Palm Beach

Near the shops on the Pittwater side of *Palm Beach*, ferries cross to secluded beaches on the west side of Pittwater and cruise boats depart to ply the Hawkesbury River system.

A brisk half-hour walk from the flying boat jetty north on Barrenjoey Beach to a walking track, following the route of an old horse drawn railway, takes you up to the light house on the top of *Barrenjoey Head*. From the Head there are fantastic views looking south to the Peninsula of Palm Beach, and north to Broken Bay, the entrance to the Hawkesbury River system.

Colonial Architect *James Barnet* designed the 11 metre high lighthouse, completed in 1881. The first lighthouse keeper, George Mulhall, died after being struck by lightning while he was collecting firewood during a storm. By rummaging around in the bush on the ocean side of the Head, east of the lighthouse, you will find his grave.

The Northern Beaches

Back at Palm Beach you can take the seaplane to return to Rose Bay, take the 190 bus that runs the 39 kilometres to Wynyard Station in the city, or take a cab back to the city along a more meandering route than the bus, to see the rest of the northern beaches that we missed on Thursday.

If you decide to take up the last option, start at *Governor Phillip Park* on Barrenjoey Road, stay on Ocean Road as it follows Palm Beach, turn right onto Palm Beach Road, then left into Florida Road. Florida Road winds past *Wiltshire* and *Hordern Parks*,

Point Piper (top left) was named after Captain John Piper, Collector of Customs, who took a percentage of wharf fees charged to ships for using docks and other facilities. Piper did very well, he built a big house on Point Piper where he entertained lavishly, he owned for a time Vaucluse House on the other side of Rose Bay, and Argyle Stores in The Rocks. In 1825 Piper was sacked by Governor Darling for failing to account for a fortune in missing customs dues. He tried to commit suicide by jumping from his boat off Point Piper, but was hauled out of the water by his servants and lived on to the ripe old age of 78.

One of Aquatic Airways' flying boats over Pittwater (bottom left). Photograph by Ron Israel, picture by courtesy of Aquatic Airways.

Whale Beach (centre) with Pittwater and Ku-ring-gai Chase National Park beyond.

Avalon Beach (above) was named by Arthur Small, a real estate agent who sold blocks of land in the area in the 1920s.

Bilgola Beach (top right). Government surveyor James Meehan called the beach 'Belgoula' in 1814, from an aboriginal word meaning swirling waters.

131

Newport Beach (above left).

Bungan Beach (far left) is quiet even on the hottest summer days because the only access to the beach is by two long steep tracks.

Mona Vale Beach and Bongin Bay in the foreground, with Pittwater in the distance (above).

The Wakehurst Parkway, opened March 1946 (left), named after Lord Wakehurst, Governor of New South Wales 1937-46, runs through 25 square kilometres of undeveloped bushland.

Houses at Castlecrag on Middle Harbour (above).

Rearing above the road like the boundary of some medieval kingdom, Northbridge (right) was built as a private venture in 1889 by the North Sydney Tramway and Development Company to help sell real estate on the far side of Salt Pan Cove. The original suspension bridge was condemned in 1936, and the present reinforced concrete bridge retaining the original battlemented towers, was opened in 1939.

pentine, which, just like a serpent, winds round and down through a palm grove past *Bilgola Beach* and up and round again to rejoin Barrenjoey Road.

Stay on Barrenjoey Road past *Newport Beach* and take Hillcrest Avenue, the eighth turn on the left, leading to *Mona Vale Headland Reserve*. From the Reserve there are great views right along Mona Vale Beach on one side, and to quiet *Bungan Beach* on the other.

The Wakehurst Parkway

Backtrack to Barrenjoey Road, which soon runs into Pittwater Road at Mona Vale. Stay on Pittwater Road through several sets of traffic lights then fork right at *Narrabeen Lakes* onto the *Wakehurst Parkway*, following a signpost for Sydney. The Wakehurst Parkway follows a picturesque route along the shore of *Narrabeen Lagoon* then through unspoilt bushland to a main intersection at *Warringah Road*.

Turn right at Warringah Road, through the suburbs of French's Forest and Forestville, cross Middle Harbour over the *Roseville Bridge*, then at the second set of traffic lights after crossing the bridge, fork left onto *Eastern Valley Way*. Following Eastern Valley Way for some kilometres as it gently winds and undulates through the suburbs of Castle Cove and Castlecrag, cross the castellated *Cammeray Bridge* at Northbridge and at the second set of traffic lights after the bridge, turn left onto the main Expressway over the Harbour Bridge and back to the city.

Tonight, to cap off an exciting week, why not treat yourself to an evening meal at the *Bennelong Restaurant* at the Opera House. You can make a booking on 250 7578. The food is good and the setting unique.

filled with palm groves overlooking the southern end of Palm Beach, then joins Whale Beach Road, with glimpses through the trees on your left of the ocean and Palm Beach. As Whale Beach Road rounds Little Head there's a good view of *Whale Beach* down below.

Stay on Whale Beach Road, turn left on Barrenjoey Road at the 'T' junction and follow Barrenjoey Road for one or two kilometres to *Avalon Beach*. It's not possible to see Avalon Beach from the road, turn left at the traffic lights near the petrol station into Surfside Avenue to look down onto the relatively unspoilt stretch of Avalon Beach.

Rejoining Barrenjoey Road, turn left after a kilometre into The Ser-

Following page:
The Bradfield Highway at dusk.

135

MAP SECTION
LEGENDS AND SCALES

MAPS 1 and 2

NATIONAL ROUTES

STATE ROUTES

HIGHWAYS

MAIN ROADS

CONNECTING ROADS

OTHER ROADS

RAILWAYS & STATIONS

PARKS & RESERVES

POINTS OF INTEREST

SCALE

0 1 2 3 4 5 km

MAPS 3 to 19

FREEWAYS .... WESTERN FWY

HIGHWAYS .... PACIFIC HWY

MAIN ROADS .... PITT ST

CONNECTING ROADS .... BEACH RD

NATIONAL and STATE ROUTE NUMBERS 1   1

OTHER ROADS (One Way Arrows) .... HUNTER ⟶ ST

UNMADE ROADS ....

TRACKS ....

RAILWAY and STATION ....

HOSPITALS (3 to 8) ....

PARKS, RESERVES, GOLF COURSES etc. ....

SCHOOLS, PLACES OF INTEREST etc. ....

SCALES ....

MAPS 3-8
0   250
metres

MAPS 9-19
0   500
metres

MAP 1

NATURE RESERVE

PACIFIC FREEWAY

Cowan

Creek

Jerusalem Bay

Porto

Creek

River

Juno Hd

Flint and Steel Bay

West Hd

Eleanor Bluff

Barrenjoe Hd

Gt Mackarel Beach

Coasters Retreat

Sandy Bch

Palm Beach

Whale Beach

BARRENJOEY

NEWCASTLE HIGHWAY

Berowra Heights

Berowra

Bobbin Head

KU-RING-GAI

Cowan

Cottage Point

Challenger Hd

YEOMANS CHASE

HEAD

Lovett Bay

SCOTLAND ISLAND

Church Point

Clareville

Careel Bay

Taylors Point

Avalon

Bilgola Plateau

Newport

Newport Beac

NATIONAL

Smiths Ck

PARK

PITTWATER

Bayview

Mona Vale

Bungan Bch

Dufty's Forest

McCARRS CREEK

Terrey Hills

Ingleside

Warriewood

Warriewood Bch

MONA VALE RD

Deep Ck

Monash Golf Course

Elanora Golf Course

North Narrabeen

Lake Park

Turimetta Hd

Narrabeen Hd

Elanora Heights

East Wahroonga

St. Ives Chase

North St Ives

Davidson

Narrabeen

Narrabeen Lake

FOREST

Collaroy Plateau

Collaroy Bch

North Turramurra

Pymble Golf C

St. Ives

Belrose

Cromer Heights

Cromer

Wheeler Heights

Narraweena

Collaroy

Long Reef Golf Course

Dee Why Lagoon

Pymble

East Gordon

Barra Brui

Davidson

Oxford Falls

Frenchs Forest

Beacon Hill

WARRINGAH

Dee Why

East Killara

Roseville Chase

Forestville

Manly Warringal War Memorial Park

Allambie Heights

Wingala

North Curl Curl

Dee Why Hd

Gordon

HIGHWAY

Lynn Ridge G.C.

Killara

East Lindfield

Davidson State Recr Area

Allambie

Brookvale

Curl Curl

West Killara

Lindfield

Killarney Heights

Wakehurst G.C.

North Manly

Queenscliff

West Lindfield

Roseville

East Roseville

North Balgowlah

Manly Vale

Manly G.

Queenscliff Bch

Nth Steyne Bch

Northern Suburbs Cemetery

Chatswood West

North Willoughby

Middlecove

Castlecove

Seaforth

Balgowlah

North Balgowlan

SYDNEY

Manly

Manly Bch

Chatswood

JOINS 2

MAP 2

JOINS

SEA

Manly
Queenscliff
Freshwater Bch
Queenscliff Bch
Nth Steyne Bch
Manly Vale
Manly G.C.
Manly Bch
North Pt
Military Res. Nat. Pk
North Hd

West Lindfield
Roseville
Killarney Heights
North Balgowlah
Roseville Chase
Castlecove
Seaforth
Balgowlah
Fairlight
Balgowlah Heights
North Reef Bch
Clontarf
North Harbour
Sydney Hbr. Nat. Pk
Sydney Hbr
South Hd

Chatswood West
North Willoughby
Middlecove
Castlecrag
Sailors Bay
The Spit
Beauty Point
Grotto Hd

Chatswood
Artarmon
Willoughby
Northbridge
Northbridge Pk
Spit Junction
Cremorne
Balmoral
Middle Hd

Lane Cove West
Naremburn
Cammeray
Mosman
Clifton Gardens
Chowder Bay
Lady June Bch
Camp Cove Bch
The Gap

Riverview
Crows Nest
North Sydney
Neutral Bay
Cremorne Point
Taronga Zoo
Watsons Bay
Sydney Hbr Nat. Pk
Bradleys Hd
Watsons Bay

Hunters Hill
Longueville
Greenwich
Waverton
Lavender Bay
Port Jackson
Nielsen Pk
Vaucluse

Woolwich
Cockatoo Is
Milsons Point
Kirribilli
Outer Sth Hd

Chiswick
Drummoyne
Birchgrove
Balmain
Millers Point
The Rocks
Farm Cove
Royal Botanic Gardens
Potts Point
Point Piper
Rose Bay
Dover Heights

Russell Lea
Rozelle
Rozelle Hospital
Pyrmont
Sydney
Woolloomooloo
Darling Point
Elizabeth Bay
Double Bay
Rose Bay

Dobroyd Point
Lilyfield
Glebe
Forest Lodge
Ultimo
Kings Cross
Darlinghurst
Bellevue Hill
North Bondi

Haberfield
Annandale
Leichhardt
Broadway
Chippendale
Surry Hills
Edgecliff
Paddington
Woollahra
Bondi

Summer Hill
Petersham
Stanmore
Camperdown
Redfern
Moore Park
Bondi Junction
Bondi Bch
Ben Buckler

Lewisham
Dulwich Hill
Enmore
Newtown
Darlington
Waterloo
Centennial Park
Waverley
Bronte

Marrickville
St Peters
Alexandria
Zetland
Randwick
Clovelly
Shark Pt

Marrickville South
Sydenham
Beaconsfield
Rosebery
Kensington
Randwick Racecourse
Coogee
Coogee Bch

Tempe
Undercliffe
Turrella
Arncliffe
Mascot
Eastlakes
Daceyville
Kingsford
Maroubra Junction
Lurline Bay

Banksia
Kyeemagh
Sydney Airport
Eastlakes G.C.
Botany
East Botany
Pagewood
Maroubra
Maroubra Bch

Rockdale
Monterey
Brighton-le-Sands
Banksmeadow
Matraville
Chifley
Malabar
Long Bay
Randwick
Anzac Rifle Range

Ramsgate
Sandringham
Dolls Point
Sans Souci
Rocky Pt
Port Botany
Yarra Bay
Phillip Bay
Little Bay
La Perouse
Long Bay Gaol
Prince Henry Hosp
Little Bay G.C.
St Michaels G.C.

Botany Bay
Towra Pt
Molineux Pt
Cape Banks
N.S.W. Golf Course
Cooks Landing Place

Premier

AMG MAG

0 1 2 3 4 5 km

MAP 3

Anzac Park

Bellevue Pk

ERNEST STREET

TRAFALGAR ST

MACARTHUR AV

ANZAC AV

Nth. Sydney Tech. College

Motor Reg.

LILLIS ST

LYTTON ST

BARDSLEY GDNS

MOODIE

ZIG ZAG L

CLARKE ST

CLARK-HUME L

WILLOUGHBY RD

ERNEST ST

SOPHIA ST

BURLINGTON ST

BURLINGTON

ALEXANDER ST

FALCON ST

FALCON ST T.A.B.

Ch of Christ

HAYBERRY ST

HAYBERRY ST

Fire Station

NICHOLSON ST

NICHOLSON PL

RIVER RD

SHIRLEY

SINCLAIR ST

MORTON

BRUCE ST

PACIFIC

Nth. Sydney Boys High Sch

KEELE ST

TUCKER ST

CARLOW

St. Leonards Park

Music Shell

North Sydney Oval

Bowls Green

CHRISTIE

HUME ST

LAMONT ST

CARLYLE

MILNER CR

GILLIES ST

ROCKLANDS

DAVID

EMMETT ST

EMMETT

BERNARD ST

MYRTLE ST

Crows Nest Boys High Sch

Mater Hospital

Nth. Sydney Girls High Sch

EDEN L

EDEN ST

HAZELBANK

CASSINS AV

RIDGE L

St. Marys Sch

R.C. Ch

SHIRLEY

BELMONT

NEWLANDS AV

ROCKLANDS

IVY ST

HAZELBANK

Brennan Park

ROAD

KING ST

McHATTON

Nth. Sydney Primary Sch

WEST ST

CHURCH ST

CUNNINGHAM

RIDGE ST

St. Thomas C of E

N. Sydney Council

Wenona Girls Sch

Noah's

N. Sydney Community Hosp.

McLAREN ST

ALFRED ST

BENT

ROSE AV

WINTER

Footbridge

WARRINGAH FREEWAY

NEWLANDS

KING

CARR ST

NEST

HARRIOTT

BAY

WAVERTON

PRIORY RD

TOONGARAH RD

EDWARD ST

BROWN ST

DOOHAT AV

ANGELO ST

BERRY ST

Monte Sant Angelo College

WARD ST

HARNETT ST

HAMPDEN ST

EATON

NOOK AV

DARLEY ST

KURRA

RAWSON

McKYE

CROWS

WHATMORE

RD

CLIFTON ST

EUROKA ST

ANCRUM ST

RILEY

OAK ST

SHORT ST

LORD ST

CHARLES

MILLER

MOUNT

Telegraph Exch.

Police Sta.

Catholic Teachers Training College

North Point

MLC Ctre

Nthside Tower

DENISON

LT. SPRING ST

SPRING

WALKER ST

LITTLE WALKER

ARTHUR ST

ALFRED ST NTH

NEUTRAL

NICHOLAS

BRAY

MARGARET

Waverton

Railway (path)

BAY

WOOLCOTT

Bowls

Waverton Park

BALLS HEAD RD

WOOD ST

LARKIN

JOHN ST

COMMODORE

BANK

BANK ST

UNION

COMMODORE ST

Graythwaite Hospital

S.C.E.G.S. (Shore)

HUNTER CR

WILLIAM

BLUE

N. Sydney

GAS

McDONALD

MOUNT

HILL ST

MALL

GLEN

WHALING RD

DORIS

HIGH

McDOUGALL

CLARK

THOMAS ST

WEBB

CHUTER

VICTORIA

HOLT ST

Pres. Ch

R.C. Ch

MACKENZIE

Private WILONA AV

C of E Ch

LAVENDER

MIDDLEMISS

WALKER L

ARTHUR ST

Park

Clark Park

HARBOUR VIEW

CLIFF

ALFRED

BROUGHTON RD

WINSLOW

WILLOU

DUMBARTON

MITCHELL ST

MUNRO

QUEENS

PRINCES

WELLINGTON

KING ST

WAIWERA

GEORGE ST

Watt Pk

LAVENDER CR

RAILWAY AV

Ramp

Lavender Bay Wharf

Lavender Bay

Ch

D.I.C.

Berrys Bay

BALLS DR

Sawmillers Res

FRENCH

WEST CRESCENT

BLUES POINT

EAST CRESCENT

BAYVIEW

MIDDLE

PARKER ST

Luna Park

BRADFIELD

FITZ

MAP 4

meray
ark
Course

GRASMERE
GRASMERE
SUTHERLAND
OAKS AV
BYRNES AV
SHORT
PARK
STREET
Bus Depot
MILITARY
BELGRAVE ST
GROSVENOR
GROSVENOR
BEN BOYD
YOUNG
COOPER
WATERS
LANE
STREET
ROAD
LANE
COOPER ST
ILLIWA ST
REYNOLDS
GERARD
BENELONG RD
JANE
ADA ST
ST
GERARD
WINNIE ST
PARRAWEEN
MONFORD PL
MILITARY
STREET
PALING ST
P.O.
MACPHERSON ST
PRINCE ST
BELMONT RD
GLOVER ST
LINDESAY
CABRAMATTA
RD
SPENCER
HOLT AV
HOLT
RANGERS
RD

CHEAT ST
LAYCOCK ST
WATSON
YEO
BOYD
ST
OLIVE ST
MAY
ROAD
YEO L
PO LANE
Fire Stn.
RANGERS
HAMPDEN AV
STREET
CRANBROOK AV
Cremorne Girls H. Sch
ALLISTER ST
EDUCAT
NORTH
SPOFFORTH
RANGERS
BRIERLEY ST
OSWALD ST
PARK AV
REGINALD ST
Reid Park
JOINS 9

HARDIE ST
BEN BOYD
BYDOWN
ST
RANGERS
HARRISON
HARRISON L
STREET
ST
RD
RANGERS RD
MURDOCH
FLORENCE
CALLIOPE ST
ORLANDO AV
ROYALIST RD
FLEET
BOYLE
HARNETT ST

PELLIER ST
LINDSAY
HIGHVIEW
RAYMOND
WESTLEIGH ST
BARRY
MILITARY
BENNETT
BURROWAY ST
BERTHA
GUTHRIE
CLAUDE AV
ROAD
SPOFFORTH
REED
BOYLE
BOYLE ST
GLENFERRIE AV
Harnett Pk
Wharf
MOSMAN AV
AVENUE

PREMIER
HIGHVIEW L
ROAD
UNDERCLIFF
RESERVE ST
RAYMOND RD
ANDERSON
Pk Bowls
SHELL COVE
POWELL
BANNERMAN
BOGOTA
PRIOR AV
MURDOCH ST
IREDALE
HODGSON
KAREELA AV
BROMLEY AV
Reserve
MCLEOD ST
TRUMFIELD L
BADHAM ST
MUSGRAVE ST

PHILLIPS ST
BOYD
HARRIETTE
AUBIN
THRUPP ST
WYCOMBE
PENSHURST AV
ROAD
HONDA
GUNDIMAINE AV
MILSON
CREMORNE
KAREELA RD
SIRIUS ST
GREEN ST
RIALTO AV
ROAD
RAGLAN ST

SPRUSON ST
BEN BOYD ROAD
MANNS AV
P.O.
WYCOMBE L
LWR. WYCOMBE RD
KURRABA
BILLONG ST
WALLARINGA AV
SPAINS WHARF RD
HOLLOWFORTH AV
SHELL
Wharf
Marina
HAYES ST

Neutral Bay
H.M.A.S. Platypus A.G.L.
ST
STANNARDS PL
Kesterton Park
Wharf
Careening Cove
ELAMANG
Loreto College
Royal Sydney Yacht Sqdrn.
PARKES ST
Wudyong Pt

Wharf
Res
Spains L'out
Lookout
BADEN RD
Kurraba Pt
Shell Cove
Reserve
ROAD
Baths
Wharf
WYARGINE AV
Mosman Bay
Wharf

MAP 5

JOINS 5

WARUNG ST
BLUES RD
HENRY LAWSON AV
Wharf
McMahons Pt

Luna Park
Pool
ALFRED ST
PAUL ST
OLYMPIC

Blues Point Res.

Blues Pt

Wharf

Sydney Harbour Bridge HIGHWAY

Port

Dawes Pt

Walsh Bay

Pier One
ROAD
1
Dawes Point Park
ROAD
Pk

Millers Pt
11

Campbells
7
Cove
6

Clyne Res.
Hbr Control Tower
TOWNS PL
DALGETY
HICKSON
MERRIMAN
BETTINGTON ST
WINDMILL
POTTINGER ST
DOWNSHIRE
FORT ST
BRADFIELD
HICKSON
Police
CIRCULAR
GEORGE
Playfair
Argyle Cntr
QUAY WST
Maritime Serv Board

Sydney Cove

Thornton Pk
DARLING ST
WESTON
St MARYS ST
EDWARD
WILLIAM ST
Illoura Res

ARGYLE
PLACE
P.O.
ARGYLE
Watson RD
Observatory Park
School
HIGH
KENT
LOWER FORT ST
TRINITY AV
DISTRIBUTOR
STREET
GLOUCESTER ST
CAMBRIDGE ST
NURSES WK
GLOBE ST
Pk
Stairs

CAHILL
CIRCULAR QUAY EXP
CIRCULAR QUAY ESP

Darling

Fire Stn.

Regent Hotel
ALFRED ST
Scout PL
ALBERT
MACQUARIE
Intercontin'l Hotel

CUMBERLAND
GLOUCESTER ST
HARRINGTON
GEORGE
HOOD PL
CRANE PL
Arbitration
MACQUARIE
LOFTUS
ST

21   20
JENKINS ST
GAS ST
6

16   15
7

17   14
8

GROSVENOR ST
YORK
LANG PL
Pk
Qantas'
BRIDGE
Lands Educ
BENT
Young
Raphael PL
FARRAR
PHILLIP
State Office Blk

CLARENCE
JAMISON
Classic
BOND
Aust. Sq.
CURTIN PL
SPRING
O'CONNELL
BLIGH
Mwth Hotel
PHILLIP

Margaret
Wynyard Park
HUNTER

Harbour

13   9
12
7
9

WESTERN
SUSSEX
Napoleon ST
KENT
SUSSEX
ERSKINE
Wynyard
CARRINGTON ST
ASH ST
ANGEL PL
PENFOLD PL
HOSKING PL
STREET

11

10

NRMA
BARRACK ST
MARTIN
G.P.O.
(Mall)
ROWE ST
CARLTON ARC
ELIZABETH
PHILLIP ST
Rail Stn.
Sydney Hospital
Mint
Hyde Park Barracks

Pyrmont Power Stn
PYRMONT
EDWARD ST
UNION ST
HARWOOD
MURRAY ST
Maritime Museum
Harbourside
PYRMONT BRIDGE
MONORAIL

10
Aquarium Site
26

KING
GEORGE STREET
PITT STREET
STRAND ARC
IMPERIAL ARC
Centre point
Mall
St.James Ch.
Law Courts
CASTLEREAGH
St.JAMES RD
PRINCE AL

Casino
MARKET STREET
City Centre
Hyde Park

JOINS 7

Mid Libr (N.S)
Parli Hous
PRINCE ALF

MAP 6
JOINS 4

COPYRIGHT: PREMIER MAPS PTY. LTD.

McBURNEY

CARABELLA

PITT
PEEL
ST

HOLBROOK

Wharf

IBILLI

WARUDA
AV
PLUNKETT
ST

MaryBooth
R.

BEULAH
ST
AV

Hosp.

Wharf

Kirribilli House

Admiralty
House

Kirribilli Hd

Jackson

Fort Denison
(Pinchgut)

Bennelong Pt.

Opera
House

Man o'War
Jetty

Mrs. Macquaries Pt.

Garden

Mrs. Macquaries
Chair

Island

overnment
House

Naval
Depot

Farm

ROAD
ROAD

Cove

Bay

1

N.S.W.
Conservatorium
of Music

Royal

Botanic

Andrew (Boy)
Charlton
Pool

Capt. Cook Dock

Kiosk

Woolloomooloo

2

MRS MACQUARIES
MRS MACQUARIES

Gardens

8
7
3

ROADWAY

WYLDE ST

AHILL EXP

Stairs

11

GRANTHAM
ST

ST. NEOT
AV

9

6

McDONALD

McDONALD
ST

Elizabeth

4

Stairs

McElhone

Bay

10

WHARF

McElhone Stairs

CHALLIS
AV

Footpath

Art
Gallery
of N.S.W.

5

LINCOLN CR

COWPER

Saint
Vincent

ROCKWALL

BILLYARD

Elizabeth Pt

ART GALLERY RD

BLAND
ST

College

ROCKWALL
CRES.

PISMO PL

Beare
Pk

Domain

NICHOLSON ST

HARNETT

ONSLOW
AV

ITHACA

RD

ESPLANADE

WILSON

NESBITT
ST

VICTORIA

Elizabeth
Bay House

Parking
Station

PLUNKETT ST

DOWLING

BROUGHAM

HORD

TUSCULUM

Macleay Pt

GRIFFITHS

McELHONE ST

PRING

ST

MANNING
ST

CRICK
AV

BOURKE
HARMER ST

ST

MACLEAY ST

MAP 7

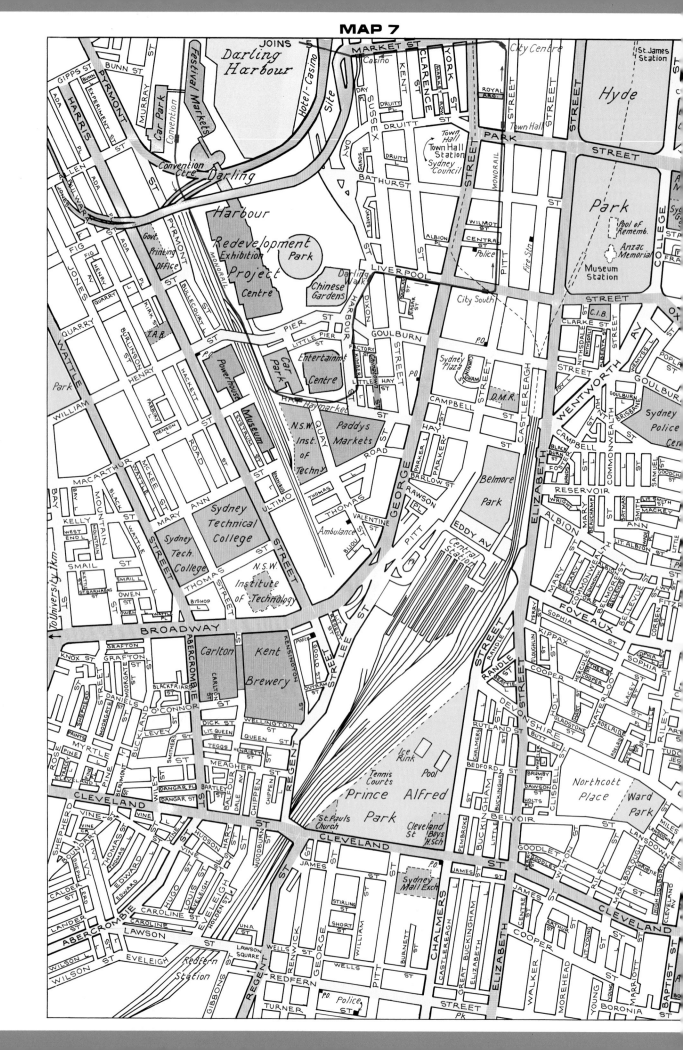

MAP 8

JOINS 6

The Domain

Rushcutter Bay

Rushcutters Bay Park

Fitzroy Gardens

St. Lukes Hosp

Mail Exch

Weigall Sports Ground

N.S.W. (White City) Lawn Tennis Association

East Sydney Tech. Coll.

Court House

Green Pk

St. Vincents Hospital

Sacred Heart Hosp.

Scottish Hospital

Glenmore Road Pub. Sch.

Royal Hospital For Women

Victoria Barracks

Town Hall

Moore Park

Sydney Sports Grd.

Driver

Kippax Lake Park

No. 2 Ground

Royal Agricultural Society Showground

Sydney Boys High School

Sydney Girls High Sch.

Sydney Cricket Ground

Parade Ring

Kings Cross

S.C.E.G.S.

Pub. Sch.

St. Margt's Hosp.

ANZAC PARADE

Street names
William, Palmer, Crown, Bourke, Forbes, Victoria, Darlinghurst Rd, Macleay, Greenknowe Av, Elizabeth Bay Rd, New Beach Rd, Oswald St, Bayswater Rd, Oxford Street, Flinders, Fitzroy, South, Dowling, Moore, Liverpool, Barcom, Glenmore, Cooper, Underwood, Paddington, Cambridge, Sutherland, Hargrave, Windsor, Hampden, Cascade, Gurner, Stewart, Regent, Victoria, Elizabeth, George, Church, Mitchell

MAP 9

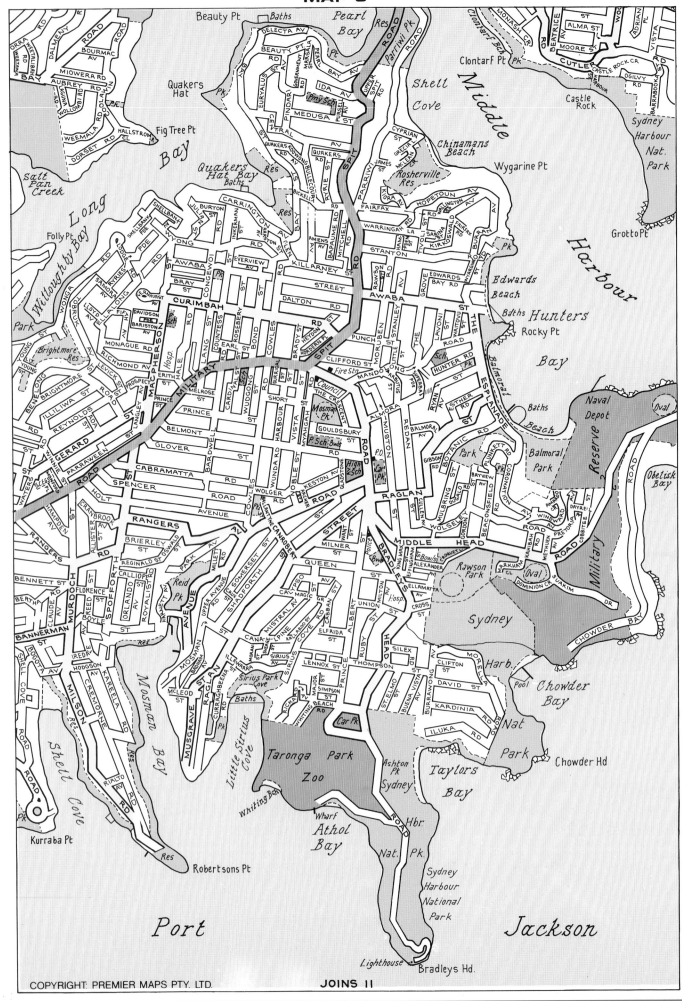

MAP 10

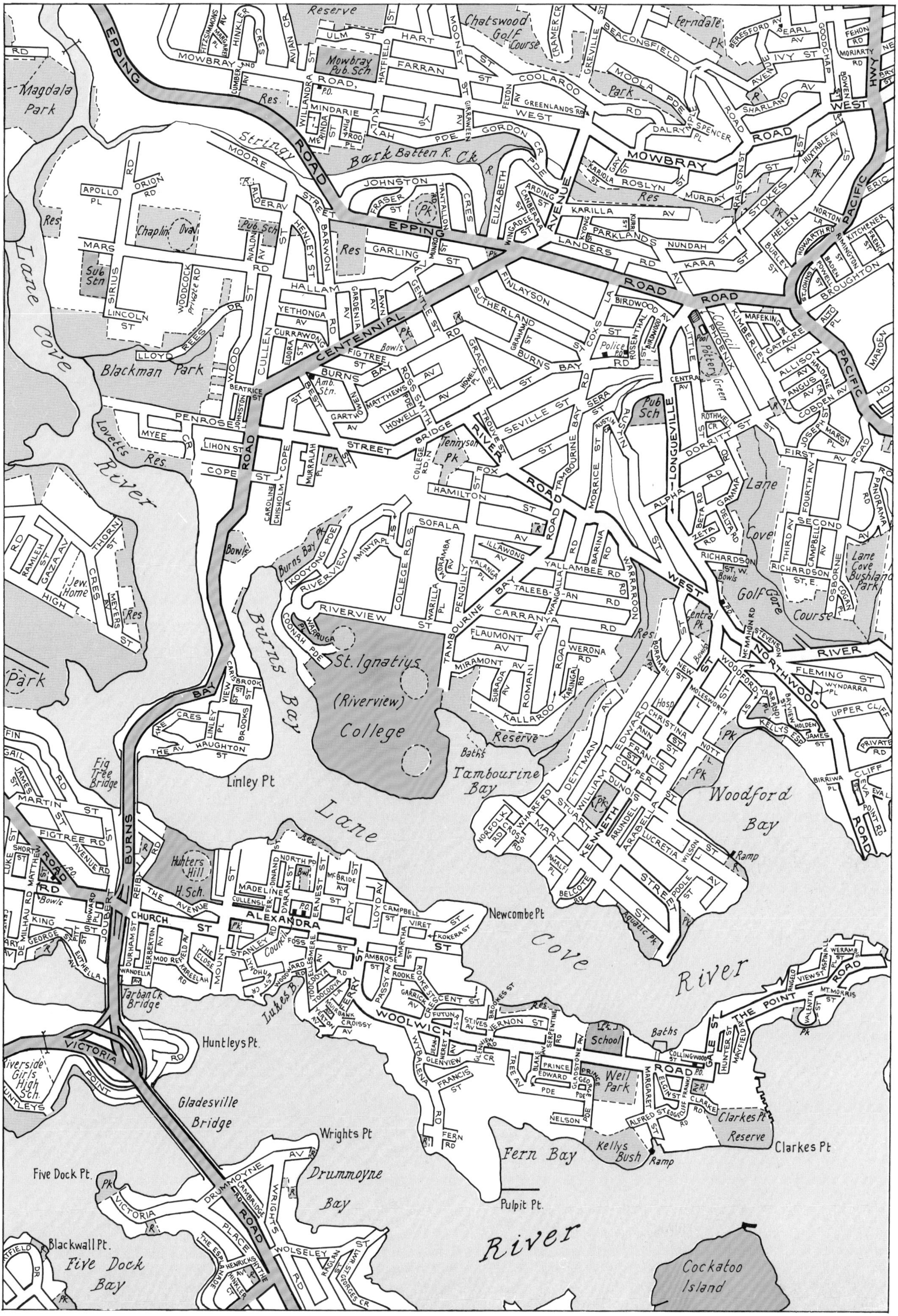

EPPING ROAD
Magdala Park
Stringy Bark Batten R. Ck
Chatswood Golf Course
Ferndale Pk
Mowbray Pub. Sch.
MOWBRAY RD WEST
MOWBRAY ROAD
PACIFIC HWY
Moola Park
Chaplin Oval
Sub Stn
Lane Cove
Blackman Park
CENTENNIAL AV
BURNS BAY RD
Lovetts River
Jew. Home
Burns Bay Pk
RIVER ROAD
Tennyson Pk
Pub Sch
LONGUEVILLE RD
Lane Cove Golf Course
Lane Cove Bushland Park
Gore Ck
St. Ignatius (Riverview) College
Burns Bay
Tambourine Bay
Reserve
Linley Pt
Fig Tree Bridge
Lane Cove River
Woodford Bay
NORTHWOOD RD
RIVER RD
Hunters Hill H.Sch.
ALEXANDRA ST
CHURCH ST
Newcombe Pt
Tarban Ck Bridge
Lukes B.
WOOLWICH RD
VICTORIA RD
Huntleys Pt.
Riverside Girls High Sch.
Gladesville Bridge
Wrights Pt
Drummoyne Bay
DRUMMOYNE RD
Five Dock Pt.
Blackwall Pt.
Five Dock Bay
Fern Bay
Kellys Bush
Weil Park
School
Clarkes Pt Reserve
Clarkes Pt
Pulpit Pt.
River
Cockatoo Island

MAP 11

JOINS 9

Sydney Harbour National Park

Shark Bay

Baths

Shark Pt.

SYDNEY HARB.

Greycliffe House

Greycliffe AV

COOLONG

Nielsen

NIRRAN

WENTWORTH

NATIONAL PARK

Park

Strickland Convalescent Hospital

Lighthouse

Bradleys Hd.

Jackson

Port

VAUCLUSE

FISHER

CARRARA

TINGIRA

Shark Id.

Hermit Bay

Hermit Pt

Res

Convent

BAYVIEW H

Clark Id

Pt. Piper

Felix Bay

Wollahra Pt

Rose Bay

DUMARESQ RD

TIVOLI

Darling Pt

WOLSELEY CR

MOSELEY

WENTWORTH PL

MUNA RD

LONGWORTH RD

Marina

CALEDONIAN RD

COLLINS

Double Bay

Blackburn Cove

WINGADAL PL

DUNARA GDNS.

ST

HEAD

Aquatic Airways

Sailing Club

VICKERY

NORWICH

SOUTH HEAD

Bay

Baths

Seven Shillings

Buckhurst AV

Council

Cranbrook School

Ramp

Lyne Pk

Tennis

KENT

Bowls

Bowls

NEW

Rushcutters Bay

THORNTON ST

SUTHERLAND CR

MITCHELL RD

GOOMERAH

St. MARKS

VICTORIA

Scots Coll.

ROSE BAY AV

ASTOR

CRANBROOK

BERESFORD

SALISBURY

POWELL

BALFOUR

O'SULLIVAN

ELANORA

MANION AV

ILUKA

Cranbrook Sportsg.

Wollahra Golf Course

NEWCASTLE

WILBERFORCE

ALBEMARLE

FARADA

Royal

Pk

WILLIAM ST

GUILFOYLE

KNOX

CROSS

GINAHGULLA RD

SHELDON

KAMBALA

RUPERTSWOOD

PLUMER

BERESFORD

Wollahra Pk

Sydney

Golf Course

ROAD

HEAD

Ascham Sch.

GREENOAKS AV

DARLING POINT

OCEAN

COOPER

HOLT

FAIRFAX

BULLARA

TIVOLI

CARRINGTON

DRUMALBYN

BALFOUR

LATIMER

BORONIA

BUNTULLA

BENELONG

South

GILG

EDGECLIFF

ALBERT

CARLOTTA

GLENMORE RD

EPPING

MALLARDY

CLARENCE

WARREN

RANFURLEY

STRATFIELD

ROSSLYN

VIVIAN

BRADLEY

LENNOX

RIDDELL

BULAND

RD

Trumper Pk

Bowls

Hosp.

Lough Pk

NORTHLAND

Cooper Park

Hosp.

BIRRIGA

HEAD

WARNE

Pk

Bowls

BEACH

LAIR

Trelawney

ROSLYNDALE

GLENCOE

OLINDEN

SUTTIE

VIEW

FLETCHER

EDWARD ST

ADELAIDE

Bellevue Pk

BANKSIA

Bellevue

FRANCIS

O'BRIEN

ROSCOE

HALL

HALL

LAMROCK

COX

Fire Stn.

WELLINGTON ST

FORTH ST

WATTUNGA

BATHURST

Pk

KANE

Bellevue

OLD

SOUTH

ACCORD AV

WATKINS

MARTINS

RICKARD AV

CASTLEFIELD

CURLEWIS

Resvr.

DR. BROOME AV

GOWRIE

SPRING

Mall

Mall

WAVERLEY

ROSE EDEN

GOWRIE

WOODSTOCK ST

KENILWORTH ST

FLOOD ST

PENKIVIL

MOORE

FOREST KNOLL AV

EDWARD

FRANCIS

MILLER AV

DENHAM

Centennial Park

OXFORD RD

GRAFTON

EBLEY

VERNON

ST

LLANDAFF

Council Waverley Park

PAUL

BONDI RD

KING ST

COULTON

ANGLESEA ST

BOTANY

PDE

IMPERIAL

CUTLER

CARRINGTON

GRAND DRIVE

LOCH

JERSEY

OXFORD ST

QUEEN

Shark Bay · Baths · Vaucluse Bay · Dunbar Hd · South Head · Hornby Lighthouse

Greycliffe House · Sydney Harb. · Nielsen Park · National Park · INSET · Lady Bay · Military Res. · H.M.A.S. Watson

Parsley Bay · Vaucluse House · Vaucluse Park · Camp Cove · Sydney Harbour National Park · Christison Park · Macquarie Lighthouse

Hermit Bay · Hermit Pt · South Head · Watsons Bay · The Gap · Pier · Baths · Gibsons · Kutti Bch · Parsley Bay

New South Head Road · Rosa Gully · Diamond Bay · Military Road · Old South Head Road

Sailing Club · Royal Sydney Golf Course · Wollahra Pk · Murriverie

High Sch · Bondi · Bondi Beach · Queen Elizabeth Pk · Bondi Bay · Ben Buckler

Sea · Tasman · Williams Pk Golf Cse · Hastings Pde E · Boulevarde

MAP 13

Resvr

Sch

MANNING ST · WARRINGAH ST · MONS RD · GLOUCESTER ST · BARDOO AV · WONGA AV · GARRAVEN AV · WOOLGOOLGA · CORAMBA ST · YAMBA · HUNTER ST · WAIMEA AV · WOODBINE · ILLAWONG · SAYERS · EILEEN ST · ST PAULS RD · WINSOME AV · FLORENCE · DAISY · BORONIA ST · MYRTLE ST

URUNGA · DORRIGO · KAMIRI ST PK · BURRINGBAR ST · BENELONG · YATAMA · KOOBILYA · BRABANOO ST · KARRI AV · MOUNTAUBAN · FROMELLES AV · BARANBALI · Pk · BARINGA · Sch

FRENCHS FOREST ROAD · BROOK ST · KEMP BRIDGE · BRIDGE · BURNT · HOPE · DUDLEY ST · SYDNEY RD

MACMILLAN · PEACOCK · REDMAN ST · REID ST · GRANDVIEW · MUNROCRASL · ADEN ST · ROSS ST · PANORAMA PDE

PONSONBY · SALISBURY SQ · PALMERSTON · ESPLANADE · BLVD · BATTLE · CRES · MANLY · AVONA · Res

Spit Bridge · Spit · Middle · ROAD · Parriwi Pk · Parrawi Pt

Pearl Bay · Pt · MARSALA · IDA AV · PURSELL ST · Pmy Sch · DUSA

Shell Cove

CYPRIAN · GRECIA · JAMES · McLLER · Rosherville Res · Chinamans Beach · Wygarine Pt

QUAKERS RD · KYRIE ST · PARRAWI RD · KIORA AV · FAIRFAX · HOPETOUN · WELLINGTON · KIRKOSWALD · SABINA

BAPAUME RD · MITCHELL · AMIENS AV · WARRINGAH LA · STANTON · GROVE · EDWARDS · BAY RD

LARNEY · AWABA · STREET · RD · THE SPIT · PUNCH · MORUBEN RD · MANDOLONG · LITTLE · HUNTER · Fire Stn · CLIFFORD ST · COUNCIL · THE CRES · ALMORA · Mosman Pk

Edwards Beach · Baths · Hunters · Rocky Pt · Bay

Castle Rock · Clontarf Pt · Pk · CUTLER · Castle Rock CR · OGILVY RD · BARRAROOK · TABALUM RD · Sydney Harbour National Park · Reef Beach · Forty Baskets Beach · Dobroyd Hd · Grotto Pt

Harbour

Cobblers Bch · Sydney Hbr · Naval · Naval Depot · Nat. Park · Middle Head · Oval · Baths

Port

KING · ARANA ST · PDE · GORDON · PARADE · BOWLS · PALM · VIEW · LAKESIDE · ROWE · Sch · PINEVIEW AV · SEEBRS · P.O. · LOVETT ST · INNES · High Sch · ADDISCOMBE · KENNETH · KOORALA ST · PARKES · BURCHMORE · LAURIE ST · FAIRWAY · Manly Golf Course · Graham Res

BALGOWLAH · DEVIATION · HAYES ST · ROSEBERY · Pk · Bowls · Club · BALGOWLAH ROAD

KITCHENER ST · PARIS ST · BRIGHTON ST · LOMBARD ST · WEST · LODGE · WOODLAND NTH · GRIFFITHS · Cemetery · HARLAND · SPRING · JAMIESON AV · BALTIC · EDWIN ST

Golf Course · Oval · High Sch · AUDREY ST · VIOLET ST · WHITE · ROAD · ANGLE ST · SOUTH STEYNE · JACKSON ST · SYDNEY · WARATAH · HILL · LA PEROUSE · AUSTIN ST · MELBOURNE · BRISBANE · COHEN · STREET · THORNTON

ETHEL · CORAL ST · PLANT ST · MARETIMO · KAREEMA · WANGANELLA · SEAVIEW · WEST ST · BEACH · PK · NEILD AV · BURTON · BENTLEY · NORTHCOTE · HILLTOP · KRUI · FAIRLIGHT · BERRY ST · Fire Stn · STREET · LAUDERDALE · WILLYAMA AV · CLIFFORD · PDE

HERNON · PERONNE AV · RUSSELL ST · NEW ST · GERTRUDE ST · HILDER ST · W · CONDAMINE · NEW ST E · GOURLAY · Marina · Wellings Res · North Harbour · Baths · BOLINGBROKE · Pool · Fairlight Bch · Delwo Bch

LINKMEAD · SANDY BAY RD · FAIRBAIRN · THE WALK · LEWIS ST · RADIO · SCALES · PDE · BINGALOE · FARRAR · VALLEY RD · GLADE ST · GLENSIDE · CONCISE · BEATTY · TITUS ST · TUTUS ST · FISHER ST · GEDDES ST

Baths · Clontarf Pk · Ramp · HOLMES AV · ALLENBY · MONASH CR · AMIENS AV · GORDON · BEATRICE · Tim Sch · RADIO · ERNEST ST · ABBOTT ST · WOODLAND ST · CURBAN · DOBROYD · BEACONVIEW RD · HEATHCLIFF · ELEVATION · Bareena Pk Bowls · NOLAN PL · BAREENA DRIVE

ADELAIDE ST · ALMA ST · MOORE ST · CUTLER · VISTA ST · WILLAWA · MULGOWRIE · Tania Pk · DOBROYD · SCENIC DRIVE

Clontarf Bch

MAP 14

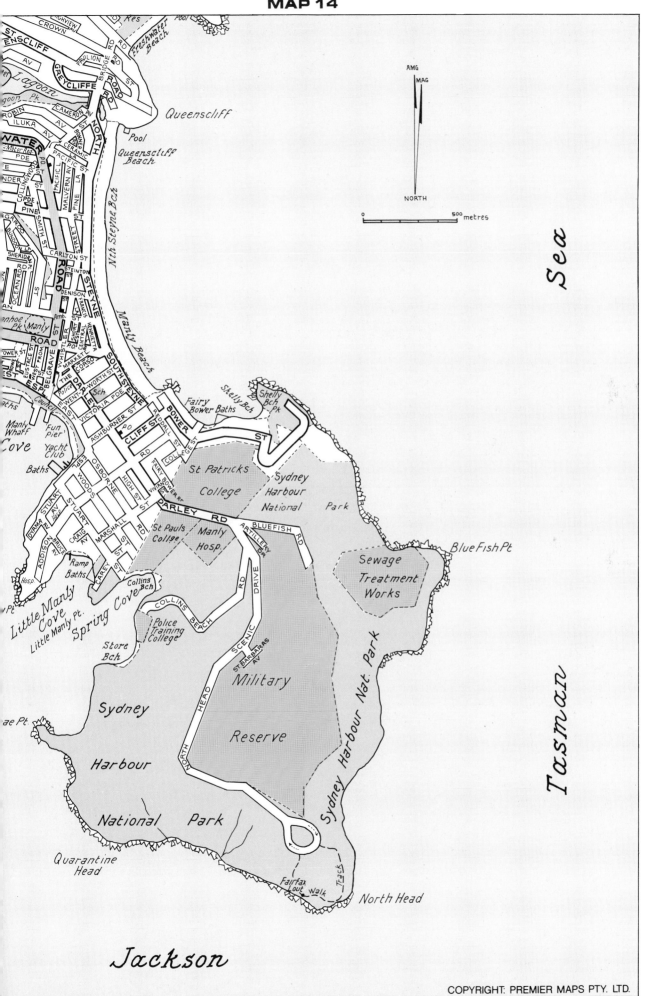

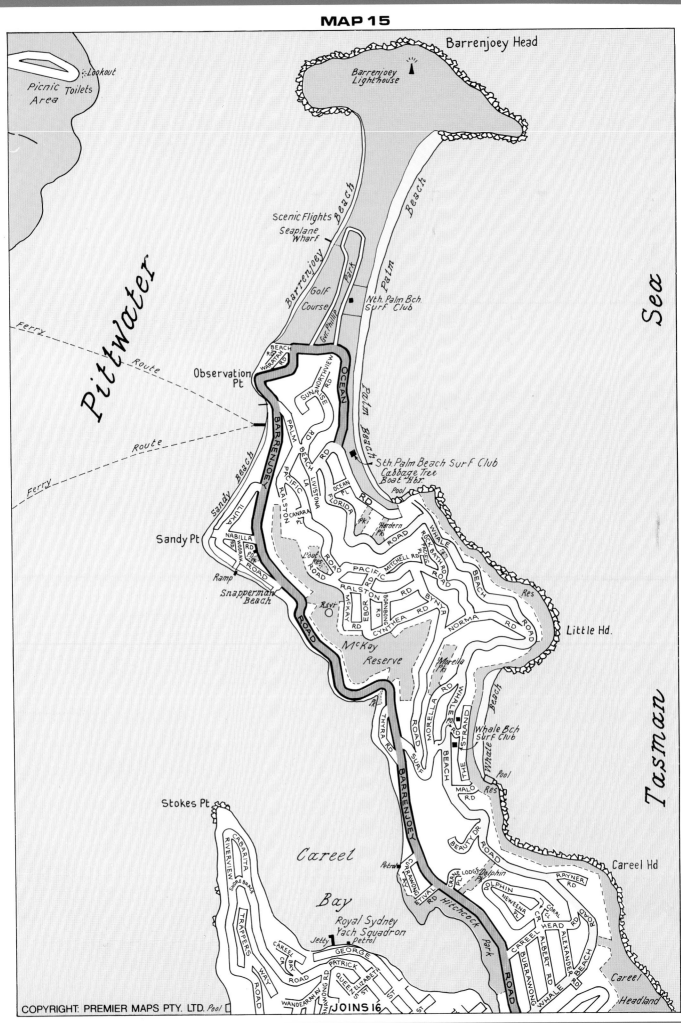

MAP 15

Barrenjoey Head

Barrenjoey Lighthouse

Pittwater

Sea

Picnic Area
Lookout
Toilets

Scenic Flights
Seaplane Wharf

Barrenjoey Beach

Palm Beach

Golf Course

Gvt. Phillip Park

Nth. Palm Bch. Surf Club

Observation Pt

Ferry Route

Route

Ferry

BEACH RD
WARATAH RD

SUNNORTHVIEW RD
SUNNRISE RD

OCEAN RD

PALM BEACH RD

PACIFIC RD
RALSTON RD

LIVISTONA LA

OCEAN FL
FLORIDA

PL

Sandy Beach

ILUKA

NABILLA RD
WOORAK RD
PALM PK

CANARA PL

D'out Res ROAD
Res ROAD

Sandy Pt

Ramp

Snapperman Beach

Rsvr

ROAD

McKAY RD
EBOR RD
CYNTHEA RD

RALSTON RD

PACIFIC RD
BOANBONG RD

BYNYA RD

MITCHELL RD

ROCK BATH RD
PACIFIC RD
WHALE RD

Sth. Palm Beach Surf Club
Cabbage Tree Boat Hbr.
Pool

Hardern Pk

WHALE BEACH

NORMA RD

ROAD

Res

Little Hd.

McKay Reserve

Morella Pk

MORELLA RD
WHALE RD
THE STRAND

WHALE BEACH

Whale Bch Surf Club

Pool
Res

MALO RD

THYRA RD

SURF ROAD

BARRENJOEY

Stokes Pt

Careel Bay

Royal Sydney Yacht Squadron
petrol

CABARITA
RIVERVIEW

SHORE BRACE

TRAPPERS

Jetty

CAREEL BAY CR

WAY
ROAD

GEORGE

PATRICK

WANDEARAWAY RD
NANWONG RD

QUEENS ST
ELIZABETH ST

Petrol

CARRAWONG AV

ETIVAL RD

BEAUTY DR

CRANE LODGE PL

Dolphin Pt

DOLPHIN CR
NEWEENA PL

CORAL CL

HITCHCOCK Park

BARRENJOEY ROAD

CAREEL HEAD RD

BURRAWONG RD

ALBERT RD

RAYNER RD

ALEXANDER RD

WHALE BEACH RD

Careel Hd

Careel Headland

Tasman

Sea

COPYRIGHT: PREMIER MAPS PTY. LTD. Pool

JOINS 16

MAP 16

Paradise Beach

Taylors Pt
Wharf

Refuge Cove

Salt Pan Cove

Green Pt
R.P.A. Yacht Co.
Royal Motor Yacht Club

Heron Cove

Crystal B.

Pittwater High Sch

Council Depot

Hudson Park

Angophora Res

Plateau Pk
Bilgola Plat Pub Sch

Crown of Newport Res

Newport Pk

Trafalgar Squ

Gladstone St

Beaconsfield St

Old Mangrove Bay

Marina

Central Park

Stapleton Park

Barrenjoey High School

Avalon Golf Course

Avalon P Sch

Surf Club

Avalon Beach

Reserve

Hole in the Wall

Head Res

Bilgola Hd.

Serpentine Res

Porter Reserve

Newport Beach

Bert Payne Park

Surf Club

Bungan Hd.

Bungan Beach

MAP 17

JOINS 16

Bayview Golf Course

Mona Vale Headland Res.

Bongin Bay

High Sch

Bus Depot

Cemetery

MONA VALE

Bowls ROAD

Kitchener Park

Mona Vale Golf Course

Mona Vale Beach

S.L.S.C.

Pool

Club

Bowls

Police

Pub Sch

P.O.

Mona Vale Hospital

FOREST RD

Church & Sch.

MACPHERSON

Old Drive In

ORCHARD ST

GARDEN ST

BOONDAH ROAD

Warriewood Beach

S.L.S.C.

Coronation

COOK TCE

PITTWATER ROAD

Warriewood Square

Soccer

Youth & Cmnty Ctr

Boondah Res.

JACKSONS RD

POWDERWORKS ROAD

Golf Driving Range

Nth. Narrabeen

Rugby Union Fields

Reserve

Turimetta Head

Turimetta Beach (Little Narrabeen)

SYDNEY

NARRABEEN

Narrabeen North Pub. Sch.

Narrabeen High Sch.

Caravan Park

Camping Area

MACKENZIE PDE

Pool

Narrabeen Head

Elanora Hts P.S.

Narroy Park

Bowls

Res.

Lake Park

Lakeside Pk.

Birdwood Pk

Beach

WAKEHURST PARKWAY

Bilarong Res.

Chattan Pk

Narrabeen Lagoon

OCEAN ST

Church Sch

JOINS 18

COPYRIGHT: PREMIER MAPS PTY. LTD.

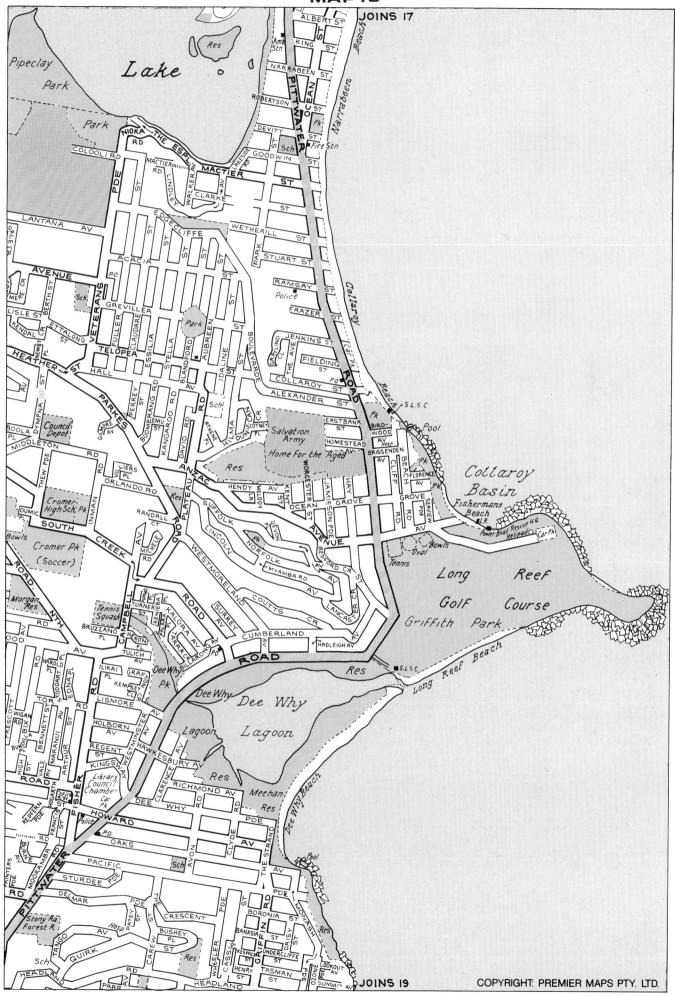

MAP18

Pipeclay Park

Lake

Res

Park

Park

NIOKA RD

THE ESPL

COLOOLI RD

MACTIER ST

MACTIER RD

LINDLEY ST

WALKER AV

CLARKE AV

LANTANA AV

EDGECLIFFE ST

ACACIA ST

GREVILLEA ST

STELLA ST

ESSILIA ST

CLAUDARE ST

Park

AVENUE

VETERANS

FULLER ST

TELOPEA

BLANDFORD ST

AUBREEN AV

IDALINE ST

BOOMERANG RD

KANGAROO RD

DAVID RD

GILMORE AV

EMU AV

ATHENE

HILMA

DUNCAN

SCOTNEY

HEATHER ST

HALL

PARKES

RD

BERTH ST

ETTALONG ST

NEWRY PL

DYMPNA ST

MIDDLETON

Council Depot

BOOLA PL

VLIERS PL

VILL PL

THEW PDE

ORLANDO RD

ANZAC

PLATEAU

RANDALL

RD

ROAD

MICHELE

CT

Cromer High Sch Pk

DUMIC PL

INMAN

SOUTH

CREEK

Cromer Pk (Soccer)

Bowls

ROAD NTH

Morgan Res

Tennis Squash

CAMPBELL

BRUZZANO PL

PIPING

TURNER ST

KENEBA

PALRA

IARRA

KILORA AV

BILLARONG AV

SURREY AV

WESTMORELAND

ROAD

COUTTS CR

MYAMBA RD

NORFOLK

LINCOLN

SUFFOLK

DEVON

Res

Pk

Res

Res

CAMERON

TULICH

ILIKAI PL

GRAF

KEMPSEY

Dee Why Pk

HOLBORN AV

REGENT ST

WESTMINSTER

HAWKESBURY AV

Lagoon

Res

Dee Why

Dee Why Lagoon

Lagoon

Meehan Res

CLARENCE

RICHMOND AV

DEE WHY

LISMORE

ARTHUR

KINGSWAY

VALE ST

HIGH ST

WIGAN

MARANUI AV

BENNETT ST

BUNDU PL

TOR ST

HAROLD PL

TODDART PL

EDNA PL

ROAD

PRESCOTT

REDFERN PDE

FRANCIS ST

HOGARTH

FISHER

HOWARD

POLICE

PO

OAKS

PACIFIC PDE

STURDEE PDE

DELMAR PDE

MOORAMBA RD

PITTWATER RD

Stony Ra Forest R

TANGO AV

QUIRK

HEADLAND

CAREW

BUSHEY PL

PARR

Sch

WHEELER

Res

KESWICK ST

CASSIA ST

HENRY ST

TASMAN ST

BANKSIA ST

BORONIA ST

CRESCENT

PATEY ST

PDE

CLYDE ST

AVON ST

THE STRAND

GRIFFIN RD

PDE

UNDERCLIFFE AV

DAISY ST

MONASH

Res

Res

EDGE

LOOKOUT AV

SUMMIT AV

OZONE

Pool

Pool

ALBERT ST

KING ST

NARRABEEN ST

ROBERTSON

DEVITT

GOODWIN

Sch

Fire Stn

Amb Stn

PITTWATER

OCEAN

Narrabeen Beach

WETHERILL

PARK

STUART ST

RAMSAY

Police

FRAZER ST

GARFLIND

THE AVE

JENKINS ST

FIELDING ST

PO

COLLAROY ST

ALEXANDER ST

EASTBANK ST

HOMESTEAD

BRISSENDEN AV

Salvation Army Home for the Aged

Res

HENDY AV

MELODY

KENT ST

OCEAN ST

WORCESTER ST

JAMIESON PDE

HAY ST

GROVE

BEDFORD CR

PYPER CR

LANCAST

CUMBERLAND

HADLEIGH AV

ROAD

Res

Collaroy (Car Pk)

ROAD

Beach

S.L.S.C.

Pk

BIRD-WOOD

Hosp

BEACH

CLIFF

GROVE RD

FLORENCE

SERVIEW AV

PDE

Pk

Pool

Collaroy Basin

Fishermans Beach

Power Boat Rescue HQ

Helipad

Car Pk

Bowls

Oval

Tennis

Long Reef Golf Course

Griffith Park

Long Reef Beach

S.L.S.C.

Dee Why Beach

MAP 19

JOINS 18

ABBOTT

Oval
John Fisher
Park
Netball
Soccer
Bowls
Weldon Pk
S.L.S.C.
Pool

Warringah Mall
Brookvale Tech.

PITTWATER

Bus Depot

WILLIAM

SHORT
WATTLE
AMOURIN
BRIGHTON

Freshwater High Sch
HARBORD
BENNETT
ADAMS STREET
Bowls
SIRGESS AV
STEWART
Curl Curl Beach
Griffin Park
Curl Curl PS.
S.L.S.C.
Pool

CONDAMINE
CORRIE

ROBERT
THOMAS
WYADRA
WELCH
OZONE
Hosp.
MARLBOROUGH
COLES
SOLDIERS
WYNDORA RD
JOHNSON ST
SURFERS PDE
WILSON ST
Park Sch
WYUNA
WYADRA
CORELLA
SEAVIEW
BEACH
Hosp.
Pool

Warringah Public Golf Course
KENTWELL RD
Bowls
Nolan Res
Passmore Res
Miller Res
CAMPBELL
GORDON
KING
INNES
LOVETT
High Sch
PARKES
BURCHMORE
LAURIE RD
KOORALA ST
KENNETH
PATON
Pk
Roseberg
Bowls
QUIRK

Manly Golf Course

MANLY ROAD
PITTWATER ROAD
LAWRENCE ST
OLIVER
DALLEY ST
QUEENSCLIFF
AITKEN AV
Hinkler Pk
Keirle Pk
Lagoon
Lagoon Pk
EUROBIN
ILUKA
GREYCLIFFE
Pavilion
BRIDGE ROAD
CAMERON
Queenscliff
Queenscliff Beach
Pool
CROWN
HIGHVIEW
Freshwater Res
Freshwater Beach
McKillop Park
Pool
EVANS

AVIATION
BALGOWLAH
WOODLAND ST
GRIFFITHS
LODGE
HAYES
SYDNEY
Harland Cemetery
Sch
LA PEROUSE
MELBOURNE
WATTLE
HILL
BALGOWLAH ROAD
Graham Res
Pool
PACIFIC
HERBERT
ARTHUR ST
FRANCIS
AUGUSTA
KANGAROO
RAGLAN
OCEAN RD
GOLF AV
ROLFE
ALEXANDER
PINE
PACIFIC
MALVERN
CARLTON ST
DENISON
STEINTON
Nth Steyne Bch
Pool

OSEDALE
LAUDERDALE AV
FAIRLIGHT
UPP CLIFFORD
THE CRESCENT
WOODS
GRIFFIN AV
ST GEORGE
JAMES ST
WEST
Ivanhoe Pk Manly
Fire Stn
Manly ROAD
BELGRAVE
Amb.
VICTORIA PDE
SOUTH STEYNE
Sch
Manly Beach
Fairy Bower Baths
Shelly Bch
Shelly Bch Pk

North Harbour
Marina
Wellings Res
NEW ST
FARRAR
VALLEY RD
GLADE ST
FISHERS
Baths
Forty Baskets Beach
Reef Beach
BOLINGBROKE
FAIRLIGHT
Pool Fairlight Bch
Delwood Bch
Marineland Baths
Manly Wharf
Manly Cove
Yacht Club
Baths
Fun Pier
Manly
COMMONWEALTH PDE
ASHBURNER
BOWER
CLIFF ST
COLLEGE
DARLEY RD
St Patricks College
St Pauls College
Manly Hosp.
Sydney Harbour National
ARTILLERY
BLUEFISH RD
DRIVE

Smedleys Pt
Manly Pt
Little Manly
Ramp Baths
Collins Bch
Police

JOINS 13

JOINS 14

COPYRIGHT
PREMIER MAPS PTY. LTD.

Acknowledgements

Many of the photos in this book are aerials, which wouldn't have been possible without Graham Gillies, Graham Gleeson and Brian Getters, the pilots at Heli-Aust who could always be relied on to position the helicopter in the right place to get the shot that was required.

While on the subject of transport, I couldn't have got to all the places on the ground without my trusty 24-year-old Holden HD. It has been round the clock at least once but has just kept on keeping on. Thank you Holden for making such a reliable car.

All the pictures except for a handful were taken on Pentax 35 mm and Pentax 6 x 7 photographic equipment over a period of 4 years. The cameras literally never let me down. Not once. Thank you Pentax for making such reliable cameras. However thanks don't go to the thief who broke into my house in May 1987 while I was dropping the kids off at school one morning, and relieved me of every camera and lens. May you rot in hell.

The film used was Kodachrome 64 in the Pentax MX and Kodak EPR 64 120 in the Pentax 6 x 7.

Great appreciation must be extended to all the people who gave me access to rooftops and balconies to take photos from. I won't name you, but you know who you are, many thanks. Thanks also to the staff at the Mitchell and State Libraries for their cooperation in making material available for copying. And thanks too to Judy at Aquatic Airways, for the loan of the slide of their seaplane.

On the production side Ian Richards turned my orginal 'rough' into a workable design, made useful suggestions in designing the type and pasted up the initial photo-stat. Meanwhile, Rosa at Deblaere Typesetting tirelessly set and re-set type as we changed and updated the text. Thank you Uncle Graham, for doing the proofreading. Max Peatman made the finishing touches to the layout, assembled the positioned prints and final type, and offered many constructive comments about books and the book trade as we slogged away to get the artwork finished and sent to the plate-makers.

Steve Seymour at Premier Maps completed the work on the maps and Face photo-headliners performed wonders on the title. I'm sure if I go to Face once more I won't have any arms or legs left.

Finally, thanks are extended to God, or whoever it was that created the natural wonder of Sydney Harbour, and to the planners, builders, engineers and architects, past and present, who built Sydney. 'Cos if it wasn't there, I couldn't have photographed it.

Index